Published by *Iskra Books* © 2025

10 9 8 7 6 5 4 3 2 1

Translated into English and edited from the Yiddish Second Revised Edition

All rights reserved.
The moral rights of the author have been asserted.

Iskra Books
iskrabooks.org
Olympia, US | London, England | Dublin, Ireland

Iskra Books is a nonprofit, independent, scholarly publisher—publishing original works of revolutionary theory, history, education, and art, as well as edited collections, new translations, and critical republications of older works.

979-8-3485-0062-7 (*Paperback*)

British Library Cataloguing in Publication Data
A catalogue record for this book is available from the British Library

Library of Congress Cataloging-in-Publication Data
A catalog record for this book is available from the Library of Congress

Cover and Interior Art by Alexander Tyshler
Cover Design by Ben Stahnke
Book Design and Typesetting by Alessandro Zancan

TRANSLATED AND EDITED BY NOAH LEININGER

MOYSHE ALTSHULER

iskra books
olympia | london | dublin

Dedicated to the working and oppressed peoples of the world who fight for socialism and liberation.
Next year in the socialist world republic!

Contents

INTRODUCTION:
READING THE *HAGGADAH FOR BELIEVERS AND HERETICS*
AS A HISTORICAL POLITICAL DOCUMENT   xi
Noah Leininger

    Struggle Against Which Enemies?   xiv

    Toward an Internationalist Socialist Horizon   xviii

    About the Translator and Translation   xx

GLOSSARY   xxi

HAGGADAH FOR BELIEVERS AND HERETICS   1

    Bdikes Khomets—Search for Leaven   2

    Seyder—Order   3

    Kadesh—Sanctification   4

    Urkhats—and Wash   5

    Karpas—Greens   6

    Yakhats—Break   7

Magid—Exodus	8
Kashes—Questions	9
Undzer Hagode—Our Haggadah	11
Korekh—Sandwich	27
Hallel—Praise	29
האַגאָדע פֿאַר גלויבער און אַפּיקאָרסים [הגדה פֿאַר גלויבער און אַפּיקורסים]	31
בדיקעס־כאָמעץ [בדיקת־חמץ]—Bdikes-khomets	32
סײדער [סדר]—Seyder	34
קאַדעש [קדיש]—Kadesh	36
אורכאַץ [ורחץ] (און װאַש)—(Urkhats (Un vash	38
קאַרפּעס [כרפס] (גרינס)—(Karpes (Grins	40
יאַכאַץ [יחץ] (צעטײל)—(Yakhats (Tseteyl	42
מאַגיד (זאָגן)—(Magid (Zogn	44
קאַשעס [קשיות]—Kashes	48
אונזער האַגאָדע [הגדה]—Unzer Hagode	54
קױרעך [כריך]—Koyrekh	84
האַלעל [הלל]—Halel	86

List of Figures

Fig. 1: *Yakhats*	7
Fig. 2: *Origin of the Passover Sacrifice*	12
Fig. 3: *Reactionary Hatred*	21
Fig. 4: *Revolutionary Love*	22
Fig. 5: *Korekh*	28

Introduction

Reading the *Haggadah for Believers and Heretics* as a Historical Political Document

Noah Leininger

In 1922, five years after the October Revolution and during the denouement of the Russian Civil War, Moyshe Altshuler's *Haggadah for Passover in Yiddish: Communist Youth Haggadah* (הַגָּדָה שֶׁל פֶּסַח אַף איוורע־טײטש: קאָמסאָמאָלישע האַגאָדע *Hagode shel pesakh af ivre-taytsh: Komsomolishe hagode*) was first published by the People's Commissariat for Education of the Ukrainian Soviet Socialist Republic, where Altshuler was a leader of the Jewish section in the Communist Party. In 1927, a revised second edition under the title *Haggadah for Believers and Heretics* (האַגאָדע פֿאַר גלויבער און אַפּיקאָרסים) *Hagode far gloyber un apikorsim*) was published in Moscow by the People's Commissariat for Nationalities. While the texts of the two Haggadahs are largely identical, it is the later edition that has been translated into English and reproduced in Yiddish with minor edits to orthography and spelling. Soviet phonetic spellings of words of Hebrew or Aramaic origin have been preserved, with YIVO standard spellings provided in brackets. Vowels and consonants are given fully "pointed" (with diacritic marks) to aid Yiddish learners. As a document first written over a century ago, this *Haggadah* is a historical document of its time and place, and modern readers will best appreciate it with knowledge of its context.

Altshuler's *Haggadah* was a product of the first struggle-filled years of socialist reconstruction in the newly-formed Soviet Union. A biting parody of a typical Passover Haggadah, he uses a form familiar to his Soviet Jewish audience to establish a ritualistic means of passing on the history of the Revolution and the crucial lessons to be retained—for example, enemies of the working and oppressed masses are likened to the plagues sent by God against the Egyptians in the Exodus story. It is at the same time an explicitly anti-religious work, an early entry in a series of Soviet campaigns against all forms of organized religion: rabbis and other religious functionaries in their role of misleading and subjugating Jewish workers are condemned and compared to Orthodox priests who sought to unite workers with their bosses in one Russian nation through the work of the Church. Nevertheless, it is a quintessentially Jewish text, woven throughout with Jewish humor and a critical approach to history, politics, and theology, and intended for a Jewish readership, with its two editions only appearing in the Yiddish language.

In her book *Soviet and Kosher,* Anna Shternshis quotes in translation an excerpt that lists the names of several counterrevolutionaries who should, like chametz, be burned in the fire of the socialist revolution. She argues that the *Haggadah* is antisemitic for comparing Zionists to the White Army and one of its several antisemitic, terrorist, pogromist leaders, Anton Denikin:

The Komsomol Haggadah combines all enemies of the Soviet regime as *khometz*, and recommends burning them. Equating antagonists who were notoriously anti-Jewish, such as the commander of the White Army Alexei [sic] Denikin, to Jewish Soviet opponents, such as Bundists or Zionists, was a popular method of Soviet propaganda. It was not important why or how but simply that they were portrayed as equally obnoxious [...] Judaism was now seen not just as a religion but rather as a banner under which all Soviet enemies were united. In other words, from an anti-Judaic piece of propaganda, the Red Haggadah eventually became anti-Jewish in general.[1]

By arguing that "it was not important why or how" certain Soviet Jews were listed as enemies of the Revolution, Shternshis erases the political line of Altshuler's work, which is firmly anti-Zionist and anti-religious, but not at all antisemitic or "anti-Jewish in general." Condemning anti-worker politics from other Jews is not antisemitic. Nothing in Altshuler's *Haggadah* implies hostility to Jewish people "in general," as she asserts, and nowhere is Judaism attacked as "a banner under which all Soviet enemies were united," which is an incredible allegation that finds no basis in his text; no second work is cited to suggest another source to support this claim. Indeed, Shternshis admits that Soviet "anti-Passover ventures used to coincide with the 'mainstream' campaign against Easter," which implies there was no special hostility to Judaism.[2]

---

1 Anna Shternshis, *Soviet and Kosher: Jewish Popular Culture in the Soviet Union, 1923–1939* (Indiana University Press, 2006), 27–28, 33–34. Shternshis introduces the *Haggadah* as Altshuler's *Komsomolishe hagode*, but gives a citation for *Hagode far gloyber un apikorsim* in the endnotes. Some sources place the publication of the *Komsomolishe hagode* in 1930, three years after *Hagode far gloyber un apikorsim*; the Russian State Library catalog lists a publication date of 1922. The earlier date comports better with that edition's text, which begins, "Five years after the first Komsomol Passover [...]." Since the text of the two Haggadahs is largely identical, it is likely that the 1927 "revised second edition" is a revision of an earlier *Komsomolishe hagode*.

2 Anna Shternshis, "אַ צולהכעיסדיקע הגדה פֿון סאָוועטישן מיליטאַנטיש אפּיקורס"

Struggle Against Which Enemies?

A quarter century before the Zionist entity was erected in occupied Palestine, Altshuler's *Haggadah* condemned Zionism as a racist, class collaborationist venture seeking to unite workers with their bosses, in spite of their opposed class interests, by manufacturing hatred against other peoples. This translation was prepared for publication as the Zionist genocide of Palestinians has entered a qualitatively new stage in response to the Palestinian resistance forces' commencement of Operation Al-Aqsa Flood in October 2023, and this revolutionary *Haggadah* appears prescient in its recognition of Zionism as an enemy of Jewish workers for its nationalist obstruction of the new proletarian internationalist society being built by the Soviets.

There are four times counterrevolutionary enemies are named in the *Haggadah for Believers and Heretics*, at points corresponding to the nullification of chametz, kiddush, recounting of the plagues, and the korekh sandwich, all found in a standard Passover Haggadah. Twelve organizations or movements are named, six of them Jewish. The Jewish Labour Bund is named, whose attempt to secure for themselves the right of exclusive representation of Jewish workers and their issues in the Russian Social Democratic Labour Party (RSDLP) at its 1903 party congress was rejected by the delegates, as are five Zionist formations: the Zionist movement generally along with the Zionist Socialist and Jewish Socialist Workers' Parties, Poale Zion (translated "Workers' Zionists"), and Tze'irei Zion ("Zionist Youth"). In addition to these organizations, twenty-four individuals are named in the *Haggadah*, all of them by last name alone. Just four of them are Jewish: Rafail Abramovich, Fyodor Dan, Julius Martov, and Abram Gots. Abramovich, Dan, and Martov were Mensheviks; Gots was a Social-

---

[A spiteful Haggadah from a militant Soviet heretic], *Di Pen* 35 (1998): 65–66.

ist Revolutionary—the Mensheviks and SRs, along with the Constitutional Democrats, are listed among counterrevolutionary enemies three separate times, more times than any Jewish groups.

Only six people are compared to both chametz and plagues and therefore named twice: Viktor Chernov, Anton Denikin, Abram Gots, Symon Petliura, Józef Piłsudski, and Pyotr Wrangel, who all fought against the Bolsheviks for varying reasons. Gots, the only Jewish one of these six, was a central defendant in the 1922 trial of twelve SRs for waging armed counter-revolution against the Bolsheviks during the Civil War. Chernov was a Russian SR who had participated in Alexander Kerensky's provisional government and, after the October Revolution, joined the counter-revolutionary "Committee for the Salvation of the Motherland and Revolution" led by Gots. Piłsudski, leader of the Polish Socialist Party, led a revanchist nationalist war against the Soviets; Russian antisemites Denikin and Wrangel led the pogromist White Army, while Ukrainian nationalists responsible for the deadliest pogroms were led by Symon Petliura against the Red Army in the Civil War.

As Altshuler writes in the *Haggadah*, "One of them is openly counterrevolutionary, the other passed off under a veil of socialism and democracy—all together, equal enemies of the working class." The Mensheviks and SRs were excoriated in Altshuler's *Haggadah* as among the chief enemies of the Soviet working class in their capacity as "leftist" parties that took up arms against the Bolsheviks "under a veil of socialism and democracy." As for "openly counterrevolutionary" enemies, the international fascist reaction to the socialist revolution stands out as the principal threat: while fascism is not called out by name, more White officers are named than members of any other single group Altshuler targets for criticism. He only names three SRs and three Mensheviks, but names seven White Army or White government leaders: Anton Denikin, Alexander Kolchak, Lavr

Kornilov, Pyotr Krasnov, Nikolai Chaikovsky, Pyotr Wrangel, and Nikolai Yudenich. He also names the fascist Benito Mussolini, who had been given power by the Italian king and bourgeoisie to crush the Italian Communists five years earlier.

The fascists, not the Communists, were "anti-Jewish in general," being responsible for the largest share of the terror waged against Jewish people in the Civil War. The most devastating genocide of Jewish people for contemporary readers of this *Haggadah* took the form of these terroristic massacres that killed hundreds of thousands of Jews in the territories that would become the Soviet Union, and in many cases the pretense for the violence, when it was even provided, was alleged Bolshevism or mere sympathy toward it—the Whites had pioneered the antisemitic libel of "Judeo-Bolshevism" that Goebbels and the Nazis would later make liberal use of in their own campaign of genocidal terrorism against Soviet Communists and multinational Jews alike. This did not need elaboration for an audience who had just lived through it and remembered the perpetrators, some of whom had fled to Europe or America.

Rather than Judaism being portrayed as a "banner under which all Soviet enemies were united," as Shternshis argues, the counterrevolution against the October Revolution is the glue uniting the various "enemies" of Altshuler's *Haggadah*. The fight against the Bolsheviks and internationalist revolutionary socialism, not Jewishness, is the thread that connects the White movement, Mensheviks and SRs, European social democrats and liberals, Italian fascists, and Zionists. The inclusion of so many Zionist organizations is a political charge, not as an attack on Jewish people "in general" or as Jews, but as an attack on *which Jewish groups* were leading *Jewish workers* astray in a text obviously intended for consumption by Jewish readers.

Even in 1927, when Altshuler's revised *Haggadah* was published, the Zionist project was in the process of seizing Palestine through the violent settlement of European Jews and displacement of Palestinians. Many early settlers were so-called "socialists," including members of the Zionist-Socialist and Jewish-Socialist Workers' Parties, Poale Zion, and Tze'irei Zion that Altshuler condemned as counterrevolutionaries. The forerunner of the modern Israeli Occupation Forces was the Haganah, so named to portray itself as a "defensive" militia, which had been founded in 1920. Zionist leader (and admirer of fascism) Vladimir Jabotinsky published "The Iron Wall" in 1923, in which he argued that "Instinctively [the Palestinians] understood Zionist aspirations very well, and their decision to resist them was only natural [...] they would accept Zionism only when they found themselves up against an 'iron wall,' when they realized they had no alternative but to accept Jewish settlement."[3]

Altshuler does not shy away from castigating religious functionaries, including rabbis, kosher butchers, rabbinic judges, religious teachers—along with priests, bishops, and mullahs—for their role in promoting class collaboration and nationalism. Altshuler describes the nationalist political goal of the priesthood in the *Haggadah*:

> To strengthen the love for one's own national God and thereby strengthen nationalist sentiments; to obstruct the unification of the workers of the world, of all nationalities, in the struggle against their oppressors; and to preach the unification of all classes in one whole Jewish nation around their own God—this is what the Jewish priesthood strives for, exactly how the Autocracy had aspired to unite all classes of the Russian nation around the Orthodox Church.

While elements of rabbinic tradition are lampooned or portrayed as backward, these exclusively religious functions are not condemned

---

[3] Vladimir Jabotinsky, "О железноай стене" [About the Iron Wall], *Рассвет* [Dawn], November 4, 1923, quoted in translation in Conor Cruise O'Brien, *The Siege: The Saga of Israel and Zionism* (Simon & Schuster, 1986), 175.

as the enemy of workers in the same way that the nationalist Zionist project is.

Toward an Internationalist Socialist Horizon

Altshuler's *Haggadah* was written during the time of the New Economic Policy (NEP), a program that re-established elements of private ownership and capitalist market forces to the young Soviet economy. The Communists conceived of themselves as walking a precipitously dangerous path as they sought to consolidate working-class power, defend the Revolution from domestic and international counterrevolution, and reconstruct society on socialist economic foundations after two wars and revolutions had totally disrupted regular life for years. The underdeveloped Russian economy that the Soviets inherited needed to grow rapidly to address the needs of the Soviet people, and capitalism under the control of the Communist Party was the mechanism by which this would be accomplished. The tasks before them were tremendous: as a critical part of this work, millions of working people had to be taught to read (and alphabets developed for minority languages that had not been permitted to flourish under Tsarist oppression), and at the same time, the rationales for decisions made by the Party had to be explained in terms understandable to these workers despite their lack of education under the Tsar.

This time was also a period of profound diversity of creative output. In the 1920s, in the midst of the NEP, there was active competition over what the arts, including literature, painting, architecture, and music, would look like in the Soviet socialist project. One faction represented an ultra-left tendency that viciously attacked artists outside their clique as class enemies, demanding presentation of only those works they deemed ideologically pure enough for consumption; their organizations would be liquidated in the early 1930s and replaced with Party-led unions for creative workers because their aggressive stance was repelling even workers who were sympathetic to Communism. Altshuler's work represents another option: tendentious works produced by the Party for the ideological orientation of broader audiences of workers.

The *Haggadah* is at its heart an educational text, one that disdains to conceal its views and aims, originating as a product of the Communist Youth League and first published by the Ukrainian People's Commissariat for Education. The lesson it teaches is clear: the working and oppressed peoples of the Russian Empire, the "prisonhouse of nations," burst through their prison walls and constructed a new, multinational society, and the opponents of this effort had no right to regroup and threaten to strip back the gains that had been won in the revolution. Against bourgeois nationalism, whether Russian chauvinism or Zionism, the Communists advocated for unity of the working and oppressed peoples of all nationalities. As Che Guevara would write four decades later, "Proletarian internationalism is a duty, but it is also a revolutionary necessity. This is the way we educate our people." [4] George Habash, a founder of the Popular Front for the Liberation of Palestine, concurred: "We held the 'Guevara view' of the 'revolutionary human being.' A new breed of man had to emerge [...] *This meant applying everything in human power to the realization of a cause.*" [5]

---

4 Che Guevara, "Socialism and Man in Cuba," https://www.marxists.org/archive/guevara/1965/03/man-socialism.htm.

5 George Habash, quoted in John K. Cooley, *Green March, Black September: The Story of the Palestinian Arabs* (London: Routledge, 2015), 135.

About the Translator and Translation

NOAH LEININGER is a musician, historian, and teacher in the public schools of Central Indiana. As a scholar of Soviet culture in the global class war, his work has been published in *Liberation School* ("Music, not muddle: Re-examining Soviet sounds and the socialist project") and *Contemporary Music Review* ("Soviet sounds, Communist pedagogy: lessons for today's musicians, organizers, educators"). He is a community organizer with the Indianapolis Liberation Center and the Party for Socialism and Liberation. Noah lives in Indianapolis with his wife Rachel, their daughter Esther, and their cats, Buttercup and Westley.

Noah is an amateur Yiddishist, and this work is his first translation of a long-form Yiddish text. No machine translation was used to produce the English text; any mistakes are the translator's. To aid in the translation of this work, reference was made to the 1940 *Yidish-rusisher verterbukh* (*Yiddish-Russian Dictionary*) compiled by Soviet Jewish philologists Shprintse Rokhkind and Hertsl Shkliar; the 2013 *Comprehensive Yiddish-English Dictionary* edited by Solon Beinfeld and Harry Bochner; the 2017 *Comprehensive English-Yiddish Dictionary* edited by Gil Schaechter-Viswanath and Paul Glasser; and Gennady Estraikh's *Soviet Yiddish: Language Planning and Linguistic Development*.

Glossary

bdikes-khomets Hebrew phrase meaning "search for chametz," a ritual search done ahead of Passover for remnants of leavened food left in a Jewish house. Traditionally, the family intentionally places pieces of bread to discover, which are gathered on a wooden spoon with a feather and all burned together; any chametz that might remain is "nullified" with a prayer that declares it "ownerless as the dust of the earth." In Altshuler's *Haggadah*, several different counter-revolutionary groups are likened to chametz and "burned in the fire of the revolution." See also *chametz*.

chametz Hebrew for "leaven." Refers to foods made with grain flour that has risen, like bread, which are forbidden from being consumed or even present in a Jewish home during the Passover holiday. See also *bdikes-khomets*.

cheder Literally, Hebrew for "room." Refers to a Jewish religious elementary school attended by children until their bar/bat mitzvah at 12–13. See also *yeshiva*.

etrog Hebrew for "citron," a citrus fruit used in rituals during the Jewish holiday Sukkot. See *pitom*.

four questions Asked as part of the Passover seder, these questions begin with "מַה נִּשְׁתַּנָּה הַלַּיְלָה הַזֶּה מִכָּל הַלֵּילוֹת" *ma nishtana* *halaila haze mikol halelot,*" "why is this night different from all other nights?" which a young attendee traditionally asks as a ritualized introduction to the story of the Exodus from Egypt. In a typical Haggadah, the four questions ask why: 1) On all other nights we eat chametz or matzo; on this night, only matzo? 2) On all other nights we eat any vegetable; on this night, we eat maror (bitter herbs)? 3) On all other nights, we don't dip our food even once; on this night, we dip it twice? 4) On all other nights, we eat either sitting upright or reclining; on this night, we all recline? The answer to these questions is "עֲבָדִים הָיִינוּ לְפַרְעֹה בְּמִצְרָיִם, *avadim hayinu le-faro b-mitsrayim,*" "we were slaves to Pharaoh in Egypt." In Altshuler's *Haggadah*, different questions are asked: 1) Is Passover not a national holiday when the Jewish nation celebrates their liberation from slavery? 2) Is it not a blunder of the Communists to ask Jewish workers to give up the Passover holiday? 3) If freedom holidays like the First of May or anniversary of the October Revolution are celebrated, why shouldn't the liberation of Egypt also be? These questions are answered with a brief history of Bronze Age nomadic West Asian peoples, the Israelite religion that developed into Judaism, and the evolution of the spring sacrificial holiday into the modern holiday of Passover.

kiddush Hebrew for "sanctification." It is a prayer said over a glass of wine to mark the holiness of holidays and Shabbat, the weekly day of rest.

korekh Literally, Hebrew for "wrap." It refers to the "Hillel sandwich" made with matzo, maror (a bitter herb, like horseradish) and charoset (a sweet mixture of fruit and nuts) that is eaten before the Passover meal is served. In Altshuler's *Haggadah*, the recipe is changed to a sandwich of Zionism placed between the Second International and League of Nations, which are to be "devoured in the worldwide revolutionary uprising of the proletariat."

machzor A prayer book for special use on the high holidays Rosh Hashanah and Yom Kippur; some have also been created for use on other holidays like Passover. See also *siddur*.

mezuzah Hebrew word for "doorpost." Refers to a piece of parchment on which an excerpt of the Torah is handwritten by an expert scribe, which is encased and affixed to the doorposts of a Jewish home in accordance with religious commandments. If a mistake is made in the creation of the mezuzah parchment, it becomes unsuitable for use and does not satisfy these commandments.

mikveh Literally, Hebrew for "collection." Refers to a pool made from naturally flowing water in which Jews must wash themselves to become ritualistically pure; for example, after menstruation or upon converting to Judaism.

pitom The fragile remnants of the flower that is found at the tip of a citron, the preservation of which is necessary for the fruit to be permissible for ritual use for the Sukkot holiday. See *etrog*.

siddur A prayer book for daily use. See also *machzor*.

yeshiva A Jewish religious secondary school attended by older children and young adults, with a focus on teaching of Jewish religious law. See also *cheder*.

YHWH The name of God in Hebrew, typically translated "Lord" in some English translations of the Tanakh and most translations of the Bible. In Jewish tradition, this name is not spoken aloud or even written outside of sacred contexts; its use in Altshuler's *Haggadah*, including the expanded form with vowels, "Yahweh," is therefore a conscious transgression of this taboo.

YIVO Institute for Jewish Research; the acronym comes from its Yiddish name (ייִדישער װיסנשאַפֿטלעכער אינסטיטוט *Yidisher visnshaftlekher institut*). "YIVO standard" Yiddish is differentiated from other forms of Yiddish by its extensive use of diacritical marks to differentiate particular letters.

Haggadah for Believers and Heretics

Bdikes Khomets—Search for Leaven

Ten years ago, the working class of Russia, with the help of the peasants, searched for leaven across the land. They have swept away all vestiges of aristocratic and bourgeois rule and have taken power into their own hands; they have taken the land from the nobility, the factories and workshops from the capitalists, and have crushed the enemies of the workers on all fronts.

In the fire of the Great Socialist Revolution, the workers and peasants have burned Kolchak, Yudenich, Wrangel, Denikin; Piłsudski, Petliura; Chernov, Gots; Dan, Martov, and Abramovich;[1] and have said a blessing:

"All the landlords, the capitalists, and their helpers—Mensheviks, SRs, Kadets, Bundists, Zionists, Zionist-Socialists, Jewish-Socialists, Workers' Zionists, Zionist Youth, and all other counter-revolutionaries—shall be burned in the fire of the revolution. No hope of recovery shall come to those who are burned; as for the remainder who survive, we forsake them and hand them over to the custody of the State Political Directorate."

---

1 In the original text, only surnames are given; full names given in notes are presumed to be the person named. Alexander Kolchak, Nikolai Yudenich, Pyotr Wrangel, and Anton Denikin were commanders of the White Army; Józef Piłsudski and Symon Petliura were nationalist counterrevolutionary leaders in Poland and Ukraine, respectively; Viktor Chernov and Abram Gots were Socialist Revolutionaries (SRs), whose party engaged in anti-Bolshevik terrorism after the revolution, including a failed assassination attempt on Lenin; and Fyodor Dan, Julius Martov, and Rafail Abramovich were Mensheviks. Abramovich was also a member of the Jewish Labour Bund, which had sought to be the sole representative of Jewish workers in the Russian Social Democratic Labour Party, which was opposed by the Bolsheviks and Mensheviks alike at the second congress of the RSDLP in 1903.

Seyder—Order

After burning the chametz, the working class goes to the seder.

They hold a seder in the land, bringing into order all the ruination caused by the counter-revolution, and make strides to reconstruct the country's economy which had been laid to waste from the time of the imperialist and civil wars.

In order to thoroughly organize the seder following all the laws of communism, it is necessary to free the land from the mildew of generations. The Communist Party and the Young Communist League take on this work together, and they arrange a seder following all the instructions of the Communist Haggadah. They recite:

Kadesh—Sanctification

Still there exists the capitalist order, still its supporters—Kadets, Mensheviks, SRs, rabbis, kosher slaughterers, rabbinic judges, religious teachers and other priestly functionaries—and we say: "סוֹף גַּנָּב לִתְלִיָּה„ *sof ganev le-tliya: the thief's end is the gallows.* **The capitalist world must perish; we, workers, are its gravediggers. You will help neither Chamberlain nor Poincaré, nor Mussolini nor the League of Nations, nor Kautsky nor the entire Second International of social-traitors.**[2]

---

2 Most likely, this refers to Austen Chamberlain, British Foreign Secretary at the time of publication (and older half brother of Neville Chamberlain, who was then only a junior minister). Also possible, but less likely when read with the *Komsomolishe hagode*, which lists then-British Prime Minister Bonar Law here instead of Chamberlain, is Houston Stewart Chamberlain, a vicious antisemite whose writings influenced Hitler's worldview and who joined the Nazi Party before his death in 1927. Raymond Poincaré was the French Prime Minister who supported the Allied anti-Bolshevik counterrevolution. Benito Mussolini was the fascist dictator of Italy. Karl Kautsky was a Social Democrat who vocally opposed the October Revolution, leading Lenin to castigate him as a "renegade." The Second International was a grouping of European socialist parties which had pledged to oppose imperialist war, but the German Social Democrats voted unanimously for war credits when World War I broke out.

Urkhats—and Wash

Worker and peasant, wash off all of the bourgeois filth; wash off the mildew of generations and say not a blessing, but a curse: devastation will come to all ancient rabbinical laws and customs, yeshivas, and cheders, which blind and enslave the people.

Karpas—Greens

Take a young, green spring twig, a hammer and sickle (don't forget to bring a rifle), and say, "The younger generation of liberated revolutionary people build a new, beautiful life, and atop the old capitalist order with its churches and synagogues we say a blessing: "בּוֹרֵא פְּרִי הָאֲדָמָה„, *bore pri ha-adama: creator of the fruit of the earth* which, in Yiddish, means: let them be buried nine cubits under the earth and bake bagels, or matzo—(may they go to hell)."

Yakhats—Break

Humankind is divided into two camps: workers and parasites.

Fig. 1: *Yakhats*

Magid—Exodus

And so says the Communist Haggadah:

"הָא לַחְמָא עַנְיָא", *ha lachma anya: this is the bread of affliction*—For poor bread, every capitalist has bought our sweat and blood. Driven by hunger, we "freely" became slaves to capital. Our Jewish masters, respectable bosses and rabbis, taught us to be patient. They wanted to convince us that we are hungry and miserable just because we are in the diaspora. They have turned their holidays into a means for blinding and enslaving the people. Instead of a real education, they have given us a siddur and machzor; instead of actual history, they have taught us the Haggadah and Books of Moses. Instead of the struggle for liberation, they have consistently maintained that "God will rescue you from exile!" For hundreds of years, they have repeated: "This year, you are here; next year, you will be in the Land of Israel."

Patience and slavery—our own bosses and rabbis taught us this. And now, when we have thrown off the yoke of our robbers and wreckers, when we build a life of liberation and gladness, when we convince ourselves that only we ourselves with our own tools can achieve the Communist order—even now, the rabbis incessantly chant their tired litanies: "This year, you are a slave; next year, in the Land of Israel, you will be the first to be freed."

Your efforts were in vain, you long frock coats: We no longer believe you. We have woken up. Go together with your masters, the capitalists, to eternal rest. Today is our time!

KASHES—QUESTIONS

Dear comrade! Allow me to ask you some questions.

For many years, during the seder I have I asked my father the "four questions," "מַה נִּשְׁתַּנָּה הַלַּיְלָה הַזֶּה מִכָּל הַלֵּילוֹת", *ma nishtana halaila haze mikol halelot: why is this night different from all other nights?* Every year, my father answers with the reply from the Haggadah, "עֲבָדִים הָיִינוּ לְפַרְעֹה בְּמִצְרָיִם", *avadim hayinu le-faro b-mitsrayim: we were slaves to Pharaoh in Egypt*, and God delivered us from his hands.

Is Passover not a true national holiday, when the entire Jewish nation celebrates their liberation from slavery? Is this not your blunder, Communists and Communist Youth, when you want the Jewish workers to give up the Passover holiday? After all, you are always teaching us to hate slavery and to fight for freedom. You celebrate such holidays yourselves, like the First of May or the anniversary of the October Revolution. As you know, you then explain the meaning of these celebrations of liberation, and all the workers go with you to demonstrations; why should the liberation from Egypt not be celebrated? **Is Passover not, then, a national liberation holiday?**

— Do you by any chance know, comrade, what is said in the Haggadah, after the first words "עֲבָדִים הָיִינוּ", *avadim hayinu: we were slaves*, with which your father started his endless answers to your constant questions?

— Yes, I know.

— Tell us, comrade, briefly, what is said in the Haggadah about the liberation of the Jewish people from slavery. Speak, comrade; let the comrades hear how the sacred stories talk about freedom and liberation.

— My father answers my four questions in Hebrew. The entire Haggadah is in Hebrew. I don't understand much that he says, but at the bottom of the page is a portion translated into Yiddish. I'll tell you briefly what it says:

The Jews were slaves to Pharaoh in Egypt. God led them out of there by great miracles. The king of Egypt, Pharaoh, was a great villain, so he did not want to liberate the Jews, and so God sent ten plagues upon the Egyptians, one after the other: Blood, frogs, lice, hail, and [...] and [...] anyway, ten plagues. The last of the plagues, the plague of the firstborn, was such a curse that the eldest son in every house died. God sent the plagues by great miracles and illusions, which our teacher Moses had demonstrated. Much is told about the plagues in the Haggadah, but I will make it brief. After the final plague, Pharaoh released the Jews. The Jews took their things from the Egyptians and ran away. They had to cross the sea. Then God performed a miracle and split the sea; the Jews went through on dry land, and the Egyptians who were chasing after them were drowned in the sea. After the Jews went across the sea by God's wonders, God led them through a desert and fed them with manna, which he would pour on them from heaven. Finally, God gave the Jews the Torah on Mount Sinai and brought them into the Holy Land.

This is, in brief, the whole tale.

Now, comrades, I will tell you our Communist "עֲבָדִים הָיִינוּ", *avadim hayinu*.

Undzer Hagode—Our Haggadah

More than 3,000 years ago, various tribes migrated to Asia who used to occupy themselves with animal husbandry, raising sheep and goats. These tribes would often invade neighboring lands. Some of them also penetrated into Egypt. Sometimes, they defeated the Egyptians; other times, they were overpowered by the Egyptians and driven off the land. Among the various bands was one nomadic tribe, the Israelites, who had roamed for a long time around the region where Mount Sinai was located. On the mountain was a volcano, which is to say, the mountain would spew forth great blazes of fire, ash, and stones. Such mountains are also now found in various countries. The wandering tribes thought of the volcano as a god—as a savage, cruel, and angry god, because it often caused them much real suffering. In a holy "psalm," this is how the revelation of the god YHWH is described:

> Then the earth did shake and quake,
> The foundations also of the mountains did tremble
> They were shaken, because He was wroth.
>
> Smoke arose up in His nostrils,
> And fire out of His mouth did devour;
> Coals flamed forth from Him.
>
> He bowed the heavens also, and came down;
> And thick darkness was under His feet [...]
>
> And the channels of waters appeared,
> And the foundations of the world were laid bare,
> At Thy rebuke, O Lord, [...] [3]

The nomadic tribes, who had very little knowledge of nature, believed that the whole desert, all of the mountains and rocks, were full of spirits from ancestors and the elders of the tribe, both good and bad. They used to treat the spirits as they did people who they revered—and of whom they were afraid. They would bribe the spirits with a prime

---

3 Psalms 18:8–10, 18:16, JPS 1917 English translation.

Fig. 2: *Origin of the Passover Sacrifice*

gift.

The wandering tribes used to be afraid of their evil gods and would bring them sacrifices, begging for forgiveness and asking them not to be so furious. **When the nomadic Israelites used to celebrate their biggest festival, the spring festival of Passover, the Israelites would bring the first-born of their goats and sheep as sacrificial offerings to their cruel God.**

But woe to the people who dared to remain in the street to see how God, the fire, would come down to eat his offerings! **The people hid in their tents in terror on Passover night. They used to spatter their thresholds and door frames with blood, because they believed this was the best way to keep their terrible God from breaking into their tents at night and annihilating the people.**

This was how the pagan nomadic tribe of Israelites celebrated their spring festival of Passover. Thus, they brought sacrifices to their God, Yahweh (YHWH), who lived on Mount Sinai.

Even now, nomadic Arab clans can be found who celebrate a spring festival like it, bringing their god a sacrifice of the firstborn sheep and goats.

Later, when the Jews moved into the land of Canaan to work the land, they began to worship their God in a new manner. Besides sheep and goats, they would offer him the fruits of the earth, which they had cultivated. **In the beautiful spring festival, when the first grains were ready there, they used to bake flat bread quickly and, with it, honor their God.**

Even later, when the priests set the Jewish God in the Temple in Jerusalem and brought him sacrifices there, they turned the spring festival into a holiday that exalted their God as a miracle worker and liberator.

The pagan offering of the firstborn sheep became a Passover sacrifice. The hastily baked bread, with which the pagans had worshiped their god, became matzo.

Quite clearly, this transformation could not have happened. **It was necessary to have a myth, one that was nice and attractive, which would exalt God and sanctify his commandments.**

The legend of the Exodus from Egypt was created.

The priests did not invent this story out of whole cloth. There were many old tales about the Jews that originated from the time when the various tribes, out of whom the Jewish people grew, led a wandering life, invading different lands and fighting with various peoples. **The priests have "revised" and "fit" various legends to their designs.** They made the God that they worshiped the protagonist of the stories they created.

From different ends of the land, the farthest-flung corners, people would walk on foot to the holy Temple with their offerings. There was a lot of work then for God's servants, the priests, and they made good money.

The further one moved forward in time from the true origin of the sacrifices and matzo, from the ancient pagan spring festival, the more the priestly caste added new myths and miracles to the holiday, the more new laws were invented for it; it has long been fixed as the greatest holiday of their national God.

In the entire imaginary tale of the Exodus from Egypt, you will find not one word about the idea that the people themselves should rise up against their oppressors—or should at least protest against their enslavement. The people merely groaned, and God heard their cries. The hero of the legend is not the people, but

God—the God of miracles and tricks, a God of wrath for those who do not serve him and of mercies for those who submit to him. A God who can suddenly inflict tremendous amounts of lice, innumerable frogs, boils all over the body, blood across the whole land. He can kill all of the young boys, make a snake out of a stick, dry out the sea all at once—pour manna from heaven, which tastes however you like: meat, fish, cheese, butter, cholent. Is this not a great God? Can anyone not fear him? Shouldn't he, such an excellent God, be loved? Is he not worthy of people bringing him burnt sacrifices as offerings?

The Temple has been destroyed, the sacrifices come to naught. God's servants, however, have remained, and are preoccupied with the faith of the people—should it weaken, God forbid, their income would shrink. Offerings are replaced with prayers, the number of commandments to God which every Jew must fulfill grows, the transgressions which risk enraging God are multiplied, and a whole hail of laws are poured out on the Jews' heads—laws about what one may do and what one must not do; what God wants to be done in morning and what at night; what kind of prayer to say when rising and what kind before laying down to sleep; what kind of blessing before eating and after finishing, what kind of blessing to say over bread, what kind to say over water; how to praise God for a potato, and how for an apple, how for kasha, how for knishes; what kind of compliments to give God for making humans a stomach, and how to praise him for making a rainbow. You must have God's blessing to have a wedding; without his permission, you cannot divorce. Only by his holy Torah may one give a child a name, and according to his commandments, the child must be circumcised; for his sake, the people must pay a rabbi to redeem their firstborn son, and they must sing hallelujahs to him; to his holy name the blessing said after defecating or urinating is dedicated; he does not want people to eat dairy for six hours after eating meat; he cannot tolerate when one confuses a utensil used for meat with one used for dairy; he wants Passover to be observed in accordance with all the laws—God forbid there should be a crumb of leavened bread in a Jewish home!

Laws without limit and without number, commandments you cannot count. Sins that cannot be listed.

And God often punishes a tiny little sin as he does a serious one. In order to save God's people from punishment for sin, which every person can commit intentionally or unwittingly, the priestly leaders, God's servants, look after them: rabbis, kosher butchers, religious judges, who know the precise details of God's law. They know what God allows and what he forbids. They teach the people God's Torah, explaining every letter of the holy law; they rule on religious questions, what is kosher and what is not, what may be done and what may not; they celebrate marriages under the canopy and write divorce decrees. They worry about the living and see that they should have a kosher mikveh. They care for the dead and provide them with a burial according to Jewish laws, with prayers of mourning, candles, and the marking of the anniversary of their death. Without a rabbi and kosher butcher, life is not life at all, because without them one could—God forbid—commit such deeds that God could never forgive: that it is right for someone to bless an etrog that lacks its pitom, that someone might love a girl without a blessing, or—I wouldn't wish this on any Jew—that one could have a totally unfit mezuzah at the door.

Today is Passover! Passover obviously will not come without the rabbi and without the butcher! How will you survive without a rabbi when you find barley in your soup? And what will you really do, if a chametz-covered gentile touches the Passover beet trough? To whom will you "sell" your leavened bread; who will provide you with charoset and shmurah matzo; and who will explain how to kasher your pans and dishes? Only the rabbi!

The pagan sacrifice to the angry god on the fire-spewing volcano Sinai; the fresh flat bread, which the pagan farmers used to bring as a gift to their god in the spring; finally, with the help of the rabbis and sages, became a holiday when not a speck of leavened bread is to be found at home, when the dishes you use all year must be carried up to the attic, when everything you have prepared to eat for the entire year may not be used, when you must burn up all chametz.

But pushing too far is dangerous. The rabbis understand that a command to burn *all* leavened bread will not be carried out by their practical community. It's too expensive a commandment for them! And who indeed would profit from such a story? The rabbis receive divine inspiration: instead of burning the chametz, he advises the people to sell it to gentiles during Passover. The entire Jewish community "sells," each one separately, chametz to the rabbi or a kosher butcher (each one onward, supposedly), and they "sell" it at last to the gentile bathhouse attendant. The rabbi and slaughterer put out very little to the original commercial operation, but rake in much more than the dupe who is drawn in by a few pennies in the mutual trick to deceive God.

But to burn remaining chametz is a commandment, and it will also be carried out. With a wooden spoon in one hand and a hen's feather in the other, the pious Jew searches in every corner for pieces of bread that they themselves had hidden just a few minutes before and, naturally, finds them. They collect the crumbs neatly together in the wooden spoon and at the same time say a blessing, praising the "Lord of the world," and the next morning they burn the spoon with the crumbs in the oven; they say, of course, yet another prayer, and again praise God, who gave to the children of Israel such a beautiful commandment as to search for and burn leavened bread.

All the commandments and their procedures are written down

with precision in the holy books. The world to come is promised for their consummation; for their neglect, the worst punishment from the great God.

Faith in God should not be weakened! God forbid his miracles should be forgotten—they must be explained anew year in and year out in full detail, in a contrived, "solemn" mood, with different ceremonies and symbolic hints.

Everything has its appointed place: the bitter herb, the charoset, the shankbone, the parsley—may God keep you from putting the shankbone where it is written for you to put the charoset! And you, well-read, should eat, lifting your glass of wine when it says so in the Haggadah, eat the bitter herb exactly the way it was when Hillel ate it when the Temple was still there. Do everything as God has commanded. God is a great, powerful miracle worker! Say the Haggadah again, and you will see what kind of God you have!

Believe in your God, believe in his miracles, in his greatness. If you will not believe or tell of his wonders, you are a wicked person! And do you know what the Haggadah commands to be done to evil people, those who do not believe in God's miracles? Knock out their teeth, the scoundrels, because they do not believe in "the Holy One, blessed be He." Tell them that if criminals like them were around in Egypt, God would not have brought them out of captivity. God loves only those who believe in his power and praise his beloved name.

Only God alone, only he personally, can bring about liberation through his great miracles: this is repeated again and again, endlessly, in the Haggadah.

How many teeth the rabbis would have to bust out (if only they were allowed!) of the wicked heretics who sing in their revolutionary song:

„און קיינער וועט אונדז ניט באַפֿרייען, ניט גאָט אַליין און ניט קיין העלד,
מיט אונדזער אייגענעם קלײי־זײַען [כּלי־זײַן] באַפֿרייען וועלן מיר די וועלט!"

*"un keyner vet undz nit bafrayen, nit got aleyn un nit keyn held
mit undzer eygene kle-zayn bafrayen veln mir di velt!"*

And no one else will liberate us, not God alone nor a hero;
with our own arms, we will liberate the world![4]

---

[4] These are the lyrics to the first half of the second verse of the Yiddish translation of "The Internationale."

God has his house. God rests in Zion—there, he promised to bring his children of Israel, only when the people are worthy of him. And those who recite the Haggadah, after they have related all of God's miracles that he performed in the Exodus from Egypt, and after they praised him and thanked him for them, after all of the compliments they made in the hallelujahs to their great, beautiful, wise, opulent and good God—after all this, they beseech him to ordain that, may they live to see the grandiose celebration "next year in Jerusalem," they will bring burnt sacrifices and spatter blood from the slaughtered sheep on the walls of the holy sanctuary.

In the twentieth century, in the time of aircraft and radio, in the epoch of socialist revolutions—pious Jews ask God to bless them so they can again bring burnt offerings!

Through imaginary stories about the Exodus from Egypt; through tall tales of supernatural wonders in which not a single educated person can believe, as they know the laws of nature and the explanations for natural phenomena; and through varied ceremonies, laws, blessings, and prayers, the clerical caste seeks to hold on to the belief in their national God.

Together with love and fear for the God of Israel, they plant hatred and disgust toward all other peoples, who do not believe in YHWH and worship other gods. When the door is opened in the middle of the performance of the seder to let in the prophet Elijah, for whom a separate glass of wine is poured, the reciters of the Haggadah ask their God to pour out his wrath on the people who do not serve him, for them to be entirely wiped off the earth.

This is how the "holy" Haggadah plants love for one's own God and hatred for foreign people.

This is the task of every religion. In the commandment to spread

HAGGADAH FOR BELIEVERS AND HERETICS 21

Fig. 3: *Reactionary Hatred*

Fig. 4: *Revolutionary Love*

hatred between different peoples, the rabbi is indistinguishable from the priest, the priest from the bishop, and the bishop from the mullah. Every one of them loyally serves their national exploitative ruling class, and they all together help to preserve the existing order of exploitation and enslavement by spreading darkness and ignorance.

The Passover holiday, which the Jewish priests and "sages" have given the appearance of a freedom holiday, has in reality been turned by them into a festival for the struggle *against* every movement for liberation by enslaved people against their enslavers. It is even told in one of the stories about the Exodus from Egypt that 30,000 Jewish heroes of the sons of Ephraim had wanted to liberate themselves from enslavement by taking up arms, God had them punished and they were massacred for it, because they had relied on their own strength and did not wait for God alone to free them.

To believe in God, rely on his holy name, hope for his grace, wait for his miracles, fear his punishment, love him for his mercy, not rely on your own powers—this is the point of all the miraculous stories. To strengthen the love for one's own national God and thereby strengthen nationalist sentiments; to obstruct the unification of the workers of the world, of all nationalities, in the struggle against their oppressors; and to preach the unification of all classes in one whole Jewish nation around their own God—this is what the Jewish priesthood strives for, exactly how the Autocracy had aspired to unite all classes of the Russian nation around the Orthodox Church.

A tale of freedom, so as to hold you longer in slavery—this is the "Haggadah of Passover."

The story of the Exodus from Egypt is a legend about God's strength, his omnipotence, miracles, and feats, a song of praise to God's power and a condemnation of humanity's own initiative and struggle for freedom!

Passover is not a holiday celebrating liberation, but a holiday of religious enslavement. We should not have such holidays. We celebrate our proletarian, revolutionary, true freedom holidays, when the people themselves awoke from the sleep into which God's servants lulled them; when they broke off the chains of slavery and oppression in which their oppressors, the capitalists and landlords, had shackled them; when the working class itself, with rifles in hand, reveals themselves as the liberators of their own class; **when they renounced imaginary national unity for the sake of the proletarian unity of all countries and peoples.**

When we celebrate our revolutionary holidays, we don't occupy ourselves with clever, pedantic arguments, like Rebe Yehuda, Rebe Yossi Haglili, Rebe Eliezer and Rebe Akiva, about the plagues sent by God against Egypt. The wise rabbis bicker about how many plagues were sent by God's finger and how many by his entire hand; how many plagues were sent on dry land and how many upon the sea, and how many thanks Jews must give to the "Lord of the world" for each plague sent against Egypt.

We tell on our holidays how difficult and thorny the path of the struggle for freedom is; how many of our best comrades perished in the prisons and on the gallows of tsarist Russia and are still dying in the "democratic" countries of Europe and America; how steadfastly and heroically the working class fought for their freedom: which party led them in the struggle and showed them the correct path to liberation, and which ones betrayed them and gave them over into the hands of their enemies. **We consider the path we have experienced in the struggle, evaluate our correct methods, condemn our mistakes and take measures so they will not be repeated.**

We also tell about the **plagues the bourgeoisie had sent against the fighting working class: Milyukov, Chernov, Kras-**

nov, Kornilov, Kerensky, Chaikovsky, Gots, Petliura, Denikin, Wrangel, Makhno, Piłsudski, Scheidemann, Noske, and Vandervelde.**[5]**

Not ten, but hundreds of such scourges! We tell about the plagues and point out: **this plague is from the Kadet party, that one from the SRs; this one from the Mensheviks, that one from the Polish Socialist Party.** One of them is openly counterrevolutionary, the other passed off under a veil of socialism and democracy—all together, equal enemies of the working class. **We point out where our enemies are and where our friends are. We sum up our latest revolutionary activity and take note of ways for further struggle.**

Instead of the crossing of the Red Sea, we tell of the heroic courage of the Red Army at **Perekop.**[6] Instead of the groans of the Jews in Egypt and God's miracle, we relate the real sufferings of the workers and peasants in their rebellion against their oppressors, their heroic fight and glorious victory.

Instead of telling the miracle of how God built his Chosen House, his Holy House in Jerusalem, we tell how workers of the USSR build socialism in a land of true freedom and equality for

---

5 Pavel Milyukov was a Constitutional Democrat (Kadet); Nikolai Chaikovsky and Alexander Kerensky were SRs; Pyotr Krasnov was a leader of the White Army and future Nazi collaborator; anarchist Nestor Makhno led the Revolutionary Insurgent Army of Ukraine against the White Army and Red Army alike; Gustav Noske and Philipp Scheidemann, German Social Democrats, bloodily suppressed the Communists; Emile Vandervelde of the Belgian Labor Party supported fighting WWI and defended the armed counter-revolution against the Bolsheviks.

6 Perekop is the isthmus, hailed as an unassailable fortress, that connects Crimea and Ukraine. The Red Army's defeat of Wrangel and his White Army at their last stand there in 1920 marked the victory of the Soviets in the south as well as a turning point in the Civil War, with the dissolution of the last major front of sustained fighting.

workers of all nations, and we call on all workers and peasants to take an active part in its magnificent construction.

Comrades, can you now compare the rabbis' Passover to the workers' First of May, the imaginary tale of the Exodus to the October Revolution?

Open up, comrades, the gates of the workers' state, and show all the workers and peasants of the whole world, who still find themselves under the yoke of capital, how we fought for our freedom and took power into our own hands. We call to all workers of the whole world: Stand up against your enemies! Liberate yourselves from your traitors! Come together with us, under the direction of the Communist International, in the decisive fight against the present capitalist world power!

At the same time, comrades, make a sandwich:

Korekh—Sandwich

Put the Second International with the League of Nations, add Zionism in between them and say, "יֹאכְלוּהוּ„, *yo'khluhu, they shall eat it*—let them be devoured in the worldwide revolutionary uprising of the proletariat.

Fig. 5: *Korekh*

Hallel—Praise

Tune: "The Internationale"

נידער מיטן שימל פֿון דוירעס [דורות]!
נידער מיט די קלעריקאַלע נאַציאָנאַליסטישע יאָנ־טוייווים [יום־טובֿים]!
זאָלן לעבן די רעוואָלוציאָנערע אַרבעטער יאָנ־טוייווים [יום־טובֿים]!

Nider mitn shiml fun doyres!
Nider mit di klerikale natsionalistishe yon-toyvim!
Zoln lebn di revolutsionere arbeter yon-toyvim!

Down with the mildew of generations!
Down with the nationalist clerical holidays!
Long live the revolutionary workers' holidays!

האַגאָדע פֿאַר גלויבער און אַפּיקאָרסים [הגדה פֿאַר גלויבער און אַפּיקורסים]

Bdikes-khomets

Mit tsen yor tsurik hot der arbeter-klas fun Rusland mit der hilf funem poyertum boydek-khomets geven in land. Er hot oysgeramt ale reshtn fun pritsisher un burzhuazer hershaft, hot ibergenumen di makht in di eygene hent, hot opgenumen di erd ba di pritsim, di fabrikn un zavodn ba di kapitalistn, er hot tseshlogn oyf ale frontn di sonim fun di arbetndike.

In fayer fun der Groyser Sotsyalistisher Revolutsye hobn di arbeter un poyerim farbrent: Koltshakn, Yudenitshn, Vrangeln, Denikinen, Pilsudsken, Petlyuren, Tshernovn, Hotsn, Danen, Martovn, Abramovitshn un hobn gemakht a brokhe:

"**Ale pritsim, burzhuyen un zeyere helfer—Menshevikes, Esern, Kadetn, Bundovtses, Tsionistn, Esesovtses, Yeesovtses, Poale-Tsionikes, Tseirey-Tsionikes un ale andere kontrrevolutsyonern—zoln farbrent vern in fayer fun revolutsye. Di, vos zaynen farbrent gevorn, zoln tsu keyn tkume nit kumen un di reshtn, vos zaynen geblibn, zaynen mir mafker un gibn zey iber in reshus fun GPU.**"

בדיקעס־כאָמעץ [בדיקת־חמץ]

מיט צען יאָר צוריק האָט דער אַרבעטער־קלאַס פֿון רוסלאַנד מיט דער הילף פֿונעם פּיערטום בוידעק־כאָמעץ [בודק־חמץ] געווען אין לאַנד. ער האָט אויסגעראַמט אַלע רעשטן פֿון פּריצישער און בורזשואַזער הערשאַפֿט, האָט איבערגענומען די מאַכט אין די אייגענע הענט, האָט אָפּגענומען די ערד בײַ די פּריצים, די פֿאַבריקן און זאַוואָדן בײַ די קאַפּיטאַליסטן, ער האָט צעשלאָגן אויף אַלע פֿראָנטן די סאָנים [שׂונאים] פֿון די אַרבעטנדיקע.

אין פֿייער פֿון דער גרויסער סאָציאַליסטישער רעוואָלוציע האָבן די אַרבעטער און פּויערים פֿאַרברענט: קאָלטשאַקן, יודעניטשן, וואַנגעלן, דעניקינען, פּילסודסקען, פּעטליורען, טשערנאָוון, האָצן, דאַנען, מאַרטאָוון, אַבראַמאָוויטשן און האָבן געמאַכט אַ בראָכע [ברכה]:

„אַלע פּריצים, בורזשויען און זייערע העלפֿער—מענשעוויקעס, עסערן, קאַדעטן, בונדאָווצעס, ציאָניסטן [ציוניסטן], עסעסאָווצעס, יעסאַוווצעס, פּויעלײַ־ציאָניקעס [פועלי־ציוניקעס], צעיריי־ציאָניקעס [צעירי־ציוניקעס] און אַלע אַנדערע קאָנטררעוואָלוציאָנערן—זאָלן פֿאַרברענט ווערן אין פֿייער פֿון רעוואָלוציע. די, וואָס זיינען פֿאַרברענט געוואָרן, זאָלן צו קיין תּקומה [תקומה] ניט קומען אין די רעשטן, וואָס זיינען געבליבן, זיינען מיר מאַפֿקער [מפקיר] און גיבן זיי איבער אין רעשום [רשות] פֿון ג.פּ.וו.״

Seyder

Nokhn farbrenen dem khomets tret tsu der arbeter-klas tsum seyder.

Er makht a seyder in land, brengt in ordenung ale tseshterungen, vos zaynen gemakht fun der kontrrevolutsye, un tret tsu oyftsuboyen di virtshaft fun land, velkhe iz khorev gevorn far der tsayt fun der imperyalistisher milkhome un birgerkrig.

Kedey ayntsuordenen dem seyder grintlekh nokh ale dinim fun komunizm, iz noytik tsu bafrayen dos land fun dem shiml fun doyres. Tsuzamen mit der Komunistisher Partey nemt zikh far der arbet der Komunistisher Yugnt-Farband un zey ordenen ayn dem seyder nokh ale onvayzungen fun der Komunistisher Hagode. Zey zogn op

סיידער [סדר]

נאָכן פֿאַרברענען דעם באָמעץ [חמץ] טרעט צו דער אַרבעטער־קלאַס צום סיידער [סדר].

ער מאַכט אַ סיידער [סדר] אין לאַנד, ברענגט אין אָרדענונג אַלע צעשטערונגען, וואָס זיינען געמאַכט פֿון דער קאָנטררעוואָלוציע, און טרעט צו אויפֿצובויען די ווירטשאַפֿט פֿון לאַנד, וועלכע איז באַרויו [חרוב] געוואָרן פֿאַר דער צייט פֿון דער אימפּעריאַליסטישער מילכאָמע [מלחמה] און בירגערקריג.

קעדיי [כדי] איינצואָרדענען דעם סיידער [סדר] גרינטלעך נאָך אַלע דינים פֿון קאָמוניזם, איז נויטיק צו באַפֿרייען דאָס לאַנד פֿון דעם שימל פֿון דוירעס [דורות]. צוזאַמען מיט דער קאָמוניסטישער פּאַרטיי נעמט זיך פֿאַר דער אַרבעט דער קאָמוניסטישער יוגנט־פֿאַרבאַנד און זיי אָרדענען איין דעם סיידער [סדר] נאָך אַלע אָנוויזונגען פֿון דער קאָמוניסטישער האַגאָדע [הגדה]. זיי זאָגן אָפּ

Kadesh

Nokh der kapitalistisher ordenung, nokh ire shtitser: Kadetn, Menshevikes, Esern, rabonim, shokhtim, dayonim, melamdim un andere kley-koydesh un zogn: sof ganev letliye—di kapitalistishe velt muz untergeyn; mir, arbeter, zaynen ire kabronim. Ir vet nit helfn nit Tshemberlen nit Puankare, nit Musolini, nit di Felker-Lige, nit Kautski un nit der gantser Tsveyter Internatsyonal fun sotsyal-farreter.

קאַדעש [קדיש]

נאָך דער קאַפּיטאַליסטישער אָרדענונג, נאָך אירע שטיצער: קאַדעטן, מענשעװיקעס, עסער, ראַבאָנים [רבנים], שאָכטים [שוחטים], דייאַנים [דיינים], מעלאַמדים [מלמדים] און אַנדערע קליי־קוידעש [כלי־קודש] און זאָגן: סאָף גאַנעװו לעטליע [סוף גנב לתליה]—די קאַפּיטאַליסטישע װעלט מוז אונטערגײן; מיר, אַרבעטער, זײנען אירע קאַבראָנים [קברנים]. איר װעט ניט העלפֿן ניט טשעמבערלען ניט פּואַנקאַרע, ניט מוסאָליני, ניט די פֿעלקער־ליגע, ניט קאַוטסקי און ניט דער גאַנצער צװײטער אינטערנאַציאָנאַל פֿון סאָציאַל־פֿאַרדרעטער.

Urkhats (Un vash)

Vash op, arbeter un poyer, dem gantsn burzhuazn shmuts, vash op dem shiml fun doyres un zog: nit keyn brokhe, nor a klole, a farvistenish zol kumen oyf ale fartsaytike rabonishe dinim un minhogim, yeshives un khadorim, velkhe farfintstern un farknekhtn dos folk.

אורכאץ [ורחץ] (און וואש)

וואש אָפּ, אַרבעטער און פּויער, דעם גאַנצן בורזשואַזן שמוץ, וואַש אָפּ דעם שימל פֿון דוירעס [דורות] און זאָג: ניט קיין בראָכע [ברכה], נאָר אַ קלאָלע [קללה], אַ פֿאַרוויסטעניש זאָל קומען אויף אַלע פֿאַרצייטיקע ראַבאַנישע [רבנישע] דינים און מינהאָגים [מינהגים], ישיוועס [ישיבות] און כאַדאָרים [חדרים], וועלכע פֿאַרפֿינצטערן און פֿאַרקנעכטן דאָס פֿאָלק.

Karpes (Grins)

Nem a yung grin friling-tsvaygl, a serp un hamer (farges nit nemen oykh a biks) un zog: Der yunger dor fun bafraytn revolutsyonern folk boyt a nay sheyn lebn, un iber der alter kapitalistisher ordenung mit ire kloysters un shuln makhn mir a brokhe "bore pri ha-adama," oyf ivre-taytsh heyst es: zoln zey lign nayn eyln in dr'erd un bakn beygl (oder matse).

קאַרפּעס [כרפס] (גרינס)

נעם אַ יונג גרין פֿרילינג־צוויגל, אַ סערף און האַמער (פֿאַרגעס ניט נעמען אויך אַ ביקס) און זאָג: דער יונגער דאָר [דור] פֿון באַפֿרייטן רעוואָלוציאָנערן פֿאָלק בויט אַ ניי שיין לעבן, און איבער דער אַלטער קאַפּיטאַליסטישער אָרדענונג מיט אירע קלויסטערס און שולן מאַכן מיר אַ בראָכע [ברכה] ,,בורא פרי האדמה [בּוֹרֵא פְּרִי הָאֲדָמָה]", אויף איווערע־טייטש [עבֿרי־טייטש] הייסט עס: זאָלן זיי ליגן ניין איילן אין דר׳ערד און באַקן בייגל (אָדער מאַצע [מצה]).

Yakhats (Tseteyl)

Me tseteylt di mentshheyt oyf tsvey lagern: oyf arbetndike un parazitn.

יאכאץ [יחץ] (צעטייל)

מע צעטיילט די מענטשהייט אויף צוויי לאגערן: אויף ארבעטנדיקע און פאראזיטן.

Magid (Zogn)

Un me zogt di Komunistishe Hagode:

Ha lakhma anya—far orem-broyt hot gekoyft yeder kapitalist unzer shveys un blut. Getribn fun hunger, zaynen mir "frayvilike" knekht bam kapital gevorn. Unzere Yidishe farzorger: sheyne balebatim un rabonim, hobn unz gelernt geduldik tsu zayn. Zey hobn unz aynshmuesn gevolt, az mir zaynen hungerik un elnt nor derfar, vayl mir zaynen in goles. Zey hobn zeyere yontoyvim in a mitl fun farfintsterung un farknekhtung fun folk farvandlt. Zey hobn unz anshtot emese bildung—a sidur un a makhzer gegebn; anshtot virklekhe geshikhte—khumesh un hagode gelernt; anshtot kamf far frayheyt, hobn zey unz shtendik ayngetaynet: "Got vet aykh fun goles oysleyzn!" Hunderter yorn ibergekhazert: Hayyor zayt ir do—iber a yor vet ir in Erets-Yisroel zayn.

Geduldikayt un knekhtshaft hobn unz unzere balebatim un rabonim gelernt. Un itst, vet mir hobn dem yokh fun unzere royber un farfintsterer aropgevorfn, ven mir boyen a lebn fun frayheyt un glik, ven mir hobn zikh ibertsaygt, az nor mir aleyn mit unzer eygenem kley-zayen veln derobern di Komunistishe ordenung,—oykh itst khazern iber di rabonim zeyer altn pizmen: hayyor zayt ir knekht, iber a yor, in Erets-Yisroel, vet ir ersht fray zayn.

Umzist dayn tirkhe, lange zhupitse: Mir gloybn dir nit mer. Mir

מאַגיד (זאָגן)

און מע זאָגט די קאָמוניסטישע האַגאָדע [הגדה]:

הא לחמא עניא [הָא לַחְמָא עַנְיָא]—פַאַר אָרעם־ברױט האָט געקניפֿט יעדער קאַפּיטאַליסט אונזער שװײס און בלוט. געטריבן פֿון הונגער, זײַנען מיר "פֿרייװיליקע" קנעכט באַם קאַפּיטאַל געװאָרן. אונזערע ייִדישע פֿאַרזאָרגער: שײַנע באַלעבאַטים [בעלי־בתים] און ראַבאַנים [רבנים], האָבן אונז געלערנט געדולדיק צו זײַן. זײ האָבן אונז אײַנשמועסן געװאָלט, אַז מיר זײַנען הונגעריק און עלנט נאָר דערפֿאַר, װײַל מיר זײַנען אין גאָלעס [גלות]. זײ האָבן זײערע יאַנטױװיעס [יום־טובֿים] אין אַ מיטל פֿון פֿאַרפֿינצטערונג און פֿאַרקנעכטונג פֿון פֿאָלק פֿאַרװאַנדלט. זײ האָבן אונז אָנשטאָט עמעסע [אמתע] בילדונג—אַ סידור [סדור] און אַ מאַחזער [מחזור] געגעבן; אָנשטאָט װירקלעכע געשיכטע—כומעש [חומש] און האַגאָדע [הגדה] געלערנט; אָנשטאָט קאַמף פֿאַר פֿרײהײט, האָבן זײ אונז שטענדיק אײַנגעטײנעט [איינגעטענהט]: „גאָט װעט אײַך פֿון גאָלעס [גלות] אױסלײזן!" הונדערטער יאָרן איבערגעבאַזאַרט [איבערגעחזרט]: הײַיאָר זײַט איר דאָ,—איבער אַ יאָר װעט איר אין ערעץ־איסראָעל [ארץ־ישראל] זײַן.

געדולדיקײַט און קנעכטשאַפֿט האָבן אונז אונזערע באַלעבאַטים [בעלי־בתים] און ראַבאַנים [רבנים] געלערנט. און איצט, װעט מיר האָבן דעם יאָך פֿון אונזערע רױבער און פֿאַרפֿינצטערער אַראָפּגעװאָרפֿן, װען מיר בױען אַ לעבן פֿון פֿרײהײט און גליק, װען מיר האָבן זיך איבערצײַגט, אַז נאָר מיר אַלײן מיט אונזער אײַגענעם קלײ־זײן [בלי־זיין] װעלן דערבארען די קאָמוניסטישע אָרדענונג,—אױך איצט באַאזערן [חזרן] איבער די ראַבאַנים [רבנים] זײער אַלטן פּיזמען [פזמון]: הײַיאָר זײַט איר קנעכט, איבער אַ יאָר, אין ערעץ־איסראָעל [ארץ־ישראל], װעט איר ערשט פֿרײַ זײַן.

אומזיסט דײַן טירבע [טירחה], לאַנגע זשופּיצע: מיר גלױבן דיר ניט מער.

hobn oyfgevakht. Gey tsuzamen mit dayn balebos, dem burzhui, in der eybiker ru. Haynt iz unzer tsayt!

האַגאָדע פֿאַר גלויבער און אַפּיקאָרסים [הגדה פֿאַר גלויבער און אַפּיקורסים]

מיר האָבן אויפֿגעוואַכט. גיי צוזאַמען מיט דיין באַלעבאָס [בעל־הבית], דעם בורושווי, אין דער אייביקער רו. היינט איז אונזער צייט!

Kashes

Tayerer khaver! Derloyb mir tsu fregn ba dir etlekhe kashes.

Shoyn a sakh yorn, az ikh freg ba mayn tatn tsum seyder fir kashes "ma nishtana halaila haze mikol halelot." Yeder yor entfert mir mayn tate dem terets fun der Hagode "avadim hayinu le-faro b-mitsrayim"—mir zaynen knekht geven ba Paren in Mitsraim, un Got hot unz oysgeleyzt fun zayne hent.

Iz den Peysekh nit keyn emeser natsyonaler yontev, ven dos gantse Yidishe folk fayert zayn bafrayung fun knekhtshaft? Iz dos nit keyn feler fun aykh, Komunistn un Komyugistn, ven ir vilt, az di Yidishe arbeter zoln zikh opzogn fun dem yontev: Ir aleyn lernt dokh shtendik faynt tsu hobn knekhtshaft un tsu kemfn far frayheyt. Ir aleyn fayert dokh azelkhe yontoyvim, vi tsum bayshpil, dem Ershtn May, oder dem Oktober-yontev. Ir dertseylt dokh dan di badaytung fun di frayheyt-yontoyvim, un ale arbeter geyen tsuzamen mit aykh oyf demonstratsyes, farvos zol men nit fayern di bafrayung fun Mitsraim? **Iz den Peysekh nit keyn natsyonaler frayheyt-yontev?**

— Veystu efsher, khaver, vos vert nokh dertseylt in der Hagode, nokh di ershte verter "avadim hayinu," mit velkhe zayn tate hoybt on zayn shtendikn terets oyf dayne shtendike fir kashes?

קאַשעס [קשיות]

טײַערער כאַװער [חבֿר]! דערלויב מיר צו פֿרעגן בײַ דיר עטלעכע קאַשעס [קשיות].

שוין אַ סאַך [סך] יאָרן, אַז איך פֿרעג בײַ מײַן טאַטן צום סיידער [סדר] פֿיר קאַשעס [קשיות] ,,מה נשתנה הלילה הזה מכל הלילות [מַה נִּשְׁתַּנָה הַלַיְלָה הַזֶה מִכָּל הַלֵילוֹת]." יעדער יאָר ענטפֿערט מיר מײַן טאַטע דעם טערעץ [תירוץ] פֿון דער האַגאָדע [הגדה] ,,עבדים היינו לפרעה במצרים [עֲבָדִים הָיִינוּ לְפַרְעֹה בְּמִצְרָיִם]"—מיר זײַנען קנעכט געװען בײַ פֿאַרען [פרעה] אין מיצראַים [מצרים], און גאָט האָט אונז אויסגעלײַזט פֿון זײַנע הענט.

איז דען פּײסעך [פּסח] ניט קיין עמעסער [אמתער] נאַציאָנאַלער יאָנטעװ [יום-טובֿ], װען דאָס גאַנצע ייִדישע פֿאָלק פֿײַערט זײַן באַפֿרײַונג פֿון קנעכטשאַפֿט? איז דאָס ניט קיין פֿעלער פֿון אײַך, קאָמוניסטן און קאָמיוגיסטן, װען איר װילט, אַז די ייִדישע אַרבעטער זאָלן זיך אָפּזאָגן פֿון דעם יאָנטעװ [יום-טובֿ]: איר אַליין לערנט דאָך ערנסטיק פֿלײַסיק צו װיסן קנעכטשאַפֿט און צו קעמפֿן פֿאַר פֿרײַהייט. איר אַליין פֿײַערט דאָך אַזעלכע יאָנטוייװעס [יום-טובֿים], װי צום בײַשפּיל, דעם ערשטן מײַ, אָדער דעם אָקטאָבער-יאָנטעװ [יום-טובֿ]. איר דערצײלט דאָך דאַן די באַדײַטונג פֿון די פֿרײַהייט-יאָנטוייװעס [יום-טובֿים], און אַלע אַרבעטער גײען צוזאַמען מיט אײַך אויף דעמאָנסטראַציעס. פֿאַרװאָס זאָל מען ניט פֿײַערן די באַפֿרײַונג פֿון מיצראַים [מצרים]? איז דען פּײסעך [פּסח] ניט קיין נאַציאָנאַלער פֿרײַהייט-יאָנטעװ [פֿרײַהייט-יום-טובֿים]?

— װײסטו עפּשער [אפֿשר], כּאַװער [חבֿר], װאָס װערט נאָך דערצײלט אין דער האַגאָדע [הגדה], נאָך די ערשטע װערטער ,,עבדים היינו [עֲבָדִים הָיִינוּ]", מיט װעלכע זײַן טאַטע הויבט אָן זײַן שטענדיקן טערעץ [תירוץ] אויף

— Ye, ikh veys.

— Dertseyl unz, khaver, in kurtsn, vos vert in der Hagode gezogt vegn der bafrayung fun Yidishn folk fun knekhtshaft. Dertseyl, khaver, zoln di khaveyrim hern, vi di heylike sforim dertseyln vegn bafrayung un frayheyt.

— Der tate entfert oyf mayne fir kashes oyf Loshn-Koydesh. Di gantse hagode iz oyf Loshn-Koydesh. Ikh farshtey a file nit, vos er zogt, nor untn in der Hagode iz alts oyf ivre-taytsh fartaytsh, oyf Yidish. Ikh vel aykh bekitser dertseyln vos dortn shteyt:

Di Yidn zaynen geven knekht ba Paren in Mitsraim. Hot zey Got aroysgefirt fun dort mit groys vunder. Azoy vi der keyser fun Mitsraim, Pare, iz geven a groyser roshe, un er hot nit gevolt bafrayen di Yidn, hot Got ongeshikt oyf di Mitsrim tsen makes, eyne nokh der anderer: blut, zhabes, layz, hogl un… un… bekitser, tsen makes. Di letste make iz geven—makes pkhoyres, dos iz aza min make, vos in yeder hoyz iz geshtorbn der eltster zun. Di makes hot Got geshikt durkh groys vunder un kuntsn, vos Moyshe Rabeynu hot bavizn. Vegn di makes vert in der Hagode zeyer a sakh dertseylt, nor ikh makh dos bekitser. Nokh der letster make hot Pare opgelozn di Yidn. Di Yidn hobn tsugenumen ba di Mitsrim zeyer guts un zaynen antlofn. Hobn zey gedarft durkhgeyn a yam. Hot Got vayter geton a nes un geshpoltn dem yam, di Yidn zaynen durkhgegangen in der trikenish, un di Mit-

דיינע שטענדיקע פיר קאַשעס [קשיות]?

— יע, איך ווייס.

— דערצייל אונז, כאַווער [חבר], אין קורצן, וואָס ווערט אין דער האַגאָדע [הגדה] געזאָגט וועגן דער באַפרייונג פון יידיש פאָלק פון קנעכטשאַפט. דערצייל, כאַווער [חבר], זאָלן די כאַוויירים [חברים] הערן, ווי די הייליקע ספאָרים [ספרים] דערציילן וועגן באַפרייונג און פרייהיים.

— דער טאַטע ענטפערט אויף מיינע פיר קאַשעס [קשיות] אויף לשן-קוידעש [לשון-קודש]. די גאַנצע האַגאָדע [הגדה] איז אויף לשן-קוידעש [לשון-קודש]. איך פאַרשטיי אַ פילע ניט, וואָס ער זאָגט, נאָר אונטן אין דער האַגאָדע [הגדה] איז אַלץ אויף איוורע-טייטש [עברי-טייטש] פאַרטיישט, אויף יידיש. איך וועל אייך בעקיצער [בקיצור] דערציילן וואָס דאָרטן שטייט:

די יידן זיינען געווען קנעכט בא פאַרען [פרעהן] אין מיצראַים [מצרים]. האָט זיי גאָט אַרויסגעפירט פון דאָרט מיט גרויס וווּנדער. אַזוי ווי דער קייסער פון מיצראַים [מצרים], פאַרע [פרעה], איז געווען אַ גרויסער רשע [רשע], און ער האָט ניט געוואָלט באַפרייען די יידן, האָט גאָט אָנגעשיקט אויף די מיצרים צען מאַקעס [מכות], איינע נאָך דער אַנדערער: בלוט, זשאַבעס, לייז, האָגל און... און... בעקיצער [בקיצור], צען מאַקעס [מכות]. די לעצטע מאַקע [מכה] איז געווען—מאַקעס פכוירעס [מכות בכורות], דאָס איז אַזאַ מין מאַקע [מכה], וואָס אין יעדער הויז איז געשטאָרבן דער עלטסטער זון. די מאַקעס [מכות] האָט גאָט געשיקט דורך גרויס וווּנדער און קונצן, וואָס מוישע ראַביינו [משה רבנו] האָט באַוויזן. וועגן די מאַקעס [מכות] ווערט אין דער האַגאָדע [הגדה] זייער אַ סך [סך] דערציילט, נאָר איך מאַך דאָס בעקיצער [בקיצור]. נאָך דער לעצטער מאַקע [מכה] האָט פאַרע [פרעה] אָפּגעלאָזן די יידן. די יידן האָבן צוגענומען בא די מיצרים זייער גוטס און זיינען אַנטלאָפן. האָבן זיי געדאַרפט דורכגיין אַ יאַם

srim, velkhe hobn nokhgeyogt di Yidn, zaynen dertrunken gevorn in yam. Nokh dem, vi di Yidn zaynen durkh Gots vunder durkhgegangen dem yam, hot zey Got gefirt durkh a midber un hot zey geshpayzt mit man, velkhn er flegt zey shitn fun himl. Dernokh hot Got gegebn di Yidn di Toyre oyfn Barg Sinai un hot zey gebrakht in Erets-Yisroel.

Ot dos iz bekitser di gantse mayse.

— Itst, khaveyrim, vel ikh aykh dertseyln unzer Komunistishn "avadim hayinu."

[ים]. האָט גאָט װײטער געטאָן אַ נעס און געשפּאַלטן דעם יאַם [ים], די ייִדן זײַנען דורכגעגאַנגען אין דער טריקעניש, און די מיצרים, װעלכע האָבן נאָכגעיאָגט די ייִדן, זײַנען דערטרונקען געװאָרן אין יאַם [ים]. נאָך דעם, װי די ייִדן זײַנען דורך גאָטס װוּנדער דורכגעגאַנגען דעם יאַם [ים], האָט זײ גאָט געפֿירט דורך אַ מידבער [מידבר] און האָט זײ געשפּײַזט מיט מאַן [מן], װעלכן ער פֿלעגט זײ שיטן פֿון הימל. דערנאָך האָט גאָט געגעבן די ייִדן די טױרע [תּורה] אױפֿן באַרג סינאַי און האָט זײ געבראַכט אין ערעץ־איסראָעל [ארץ־ישראל].

אָט דאָס איז בעקיצער [בקיצור] די גאַנצע מײסע [מעשׂה].

— איצט, כאַװײרים [חברים], װעל איך אײַך דערצײלן אונזער קאָמוניסטישן „עבדים היינו [עֲבָדִים הָיִינוּ].״

Unzer Hagode

Mer vi dray toyznt yor tsurik hobn in azye gevandert farsheydene shvotim, velkhe flegn zikh farnemen mit fitsukht (hodeven shepsn, tsign). Di dozike shvotim flegn oft zikh araynraysn in di arumike lender. Eynike fun zey zaynen oykh in Mitsraim durkhgedrungen. A mol hobn zey di Mitsrim baygekumen, a mol hobn di Mitsrim zey goyver geven un fartribn fun land. Tsvishn di farsheydene shvotim iz oykh geven a vander-sheyvet—Yisroel, velkher hot a lengere tsayt gevandert in der gegnt, vu s'hot zikh gefunen a Barg Sinai. Oyf dem barg iz geven a vulkan, dos heyst, der barg flegt aroysvarfn fun zikh groyse flamen fayer, ash un shteyner. Azelkhe barg zaynen oykh itst faran in farsheydene lender. Di vander-shvotim flegn haltn dem vulkan far a got, far a vildn, groyzamen, kaasdikn got, vayl der vulkan flegt virklekh zey onton zeyer oft fil tsores. In a heylikn "mizmur" vert azoy bashribn di antplekung fun got YHWH.

> "S'tsitert un rasht di erd,
> s'treyslen zikh fun di barg di gruntn
> un shoklen zikh, vayl in tsorn iz YHWH.
>
> A roykh geyt fun Zayne nozlekher,
> a fayer brent fun Zayn moyl,
> brenendike koyln shitn zikh fun Im.
>
> Er neygt dem himl un nidert im arop,
> a fintsternish iz unter Zayne fis,
>
> Es bavayzn zikh di kvaln fun im,
> un der grunt fun der erd vert antplekt fun
> Dayn tsorn, YHWH!"

אונזער האגאדע [הגדה]

מער ווי דרײַ טויזנט יאָר צוריק האָבן אין אזיע געוואַנדערט פאַרשיידענע שוואַטים [שבטים], וועלכע פלעגן זיך פאַרנעמען מיט פיצוכט (האָדעווען שעפּסן, ציגן). די דאָזיקע שוואַטים [שבטים] פלעגן אָפט זיך אַרײַנרײַסן אין די אַרומיקע לענדער. איינקע פון זיי זיינען אויך אין מיצראים [מצרים] דורכגעדרונגען. אַ מאָל האָבן זיי די מיצרים בײַגעקומען, אַ מאָל האָבן די מיצרים זיי גרויוואָר [גובר] געוואָרן און פאַרטריבן פון לאַנד. צווישן די פאַרשיידענע שוואַטים [שבטים] איז אויך געווען אַ וואַנדער-שײַוועט [שבט]—איסראַעל [ישראל], וועלכער האָט אַ לענגערע צײַט געוואַנדערט אין דער געגנט, וווּ ס'האָט זיך געפונען אַ באַרג סינײַ. אויף דעם באַרג איז געווען אַ וווּלקאַן, דאָס הייסט, דער באַרג פלעגט אַרויסוואַרפן פון זיך גרויסע פלאַמען פײַער, אַש און שטיינער. אַזעלכע בערג זיינען אויך איצט פאַראַן אין פאַרשיידענע לענדער. די וואַנדער-שוואַטים [שבטים] פלעגן האַלטן דעם וווּלקאַן פאַר אַ גאָט, פאַר אַ ווילדן, גרויזאַמען, קאַפּסדיקן [בעסדיקן] גאָט, ווײַל דער וווּלקאַן פלעגט ווירקלעך זיי אָנטאָן זייער אָפט פיל צאָרעס [צרות]. אין אַ הייליקן „מיזמור [מזמור]" ווערט אזוי באַשריבן די אַנטפּלעקונג פון גאָט יהוה.

„ס'ציטערט און ראַשט [רעשט] די ערד,
ס'טרייסלען זיך די בערג די גרונטן
און שאָקלען זיך, ווײַל אין צאָרן איז יהוה.

אַ רויך גייט פון זיינע נאָזלעכער,
אַ פײַער ברענט פון זיין מויל,
ברענענדיקע קוילן שטן זיך פון אים.

ער נייגט דעם הימל און נידערט אים אַראָפּ,
אַ פינצטערניש איז אונטער זיינע פיס.

עס באַוויזן זיך די קוואַלן פון אים,
און דער גרונט פון דער ערד ווערט אַנטפּלעקט
פון דיין צאָרן, יהוה!"

Di vander-shvotim, vos zaynen geven zeyer veynik bahavnt in natur-kentenish, hobn gegloybt az der gantser midber, ale berg un shteyner zaynen ful bazetst mit gayster. Mit gayster fun di oves un fun di eltste fun sheyvet: gute un shlekhte. Mit di gayster flegn zey zikh bageyn, vi mit mentshn, far velkhe me hot opshayn far velkhe me hot moyre. Zey flegn zey unterkoyfn mit a feter matone.

Di vander-shvotim flegn moyre hobn far zeyere beyze geter un flegn zey brengen korbones, iberbetn zey, zey zoln azoy tsorndik nit zayn. **Ven dos vander-folk Yisroel flegt fayern zayn grestn yontev Peysekh, dem yontev fun friling, flegn di Isreylim zeyer groyzamen Got far a korbn brengen di pkhoyrim (di ersht-geboyrene fun tsign un shepsn).**

Ober vey tsu mentshn, velkhe vagn tsu blaybn oyfn gas tsu kukn, vi Got, dos fayer, vet aropgeyn esn zayne korbones! **Di mentshn hobn in der nakht fun Peysekh fun shrek zikh bahaltn in zeyere getseltn. Di shveln un pritelkes fun zeyere tirn flegn zey bashpritsn mit blut, vayl zey flegn gloybn, az dos iz di beste trufe, az der shreklekher Got zol zikh in der nakht nit araynraysn in getselt un farnikhtn di mentshn.**

Azoy hot der getsndinerisher vander-sheyvet Yisroel gefayert zayn friling-yontev—Peysekh. Azoy hot er korbones gebrakht zayn Got Yehove (YHWH), velkher hot gevoynt oyfn Barg Sinai.

די וואנדער־שוואטים [שבטים], וואס זיינען געווען זייער ווייניק
באהאוונט אין נאטור־קענטעניש, האבן געגלויבט אז דער גאנצער מידבער
[מידבר], אלע בערג און שטיינער זיינען פול באזעצט מיט גייסטער. מיט
גייסטער פון די אָוות [אָבֿות] און פון די עלטסטע פון שייוועט [שבֿט]: גוטע און
שלעכטע. מיט די גייסטער פֿלעגן זיי זיך באגיין, ווי מיט מענטשן, פֿאר וועלכע
מע האט אפשיין פֿאר וועלכע מע האט מוירע [מורא]. זיי פֿלעגן זיי אונטערקויפֿן
מיט א בעסער מאטאנע [מתּנה].

די וואנדער־שוואטים [שבטים] פֿלעגן מוירע [מורא] האבן פֿאר זייערע
בייזע געטער און פֿלעגן זיי ברענגען קארבאנעס [קרבנות], איבערבעטן זיי,
זיי זאלן אזוי צארנדיק ניט זיין. ווען דאס וואנדער־פֿאלק איסראעל [ישׂראל]
פֿלעגט פֿיערן זיין גרעסטן יאנטעוו [יום־טובֿ] פייסעך [פּסח], דעם יאנטעוו
[יום־טובֿ] פֿון פרילינג, פֿלעגן די איסרעילים [ישׂראלים] זייער גרויזאמען גאט
פֿאר א קאָרבן [קרבן] ברענגען די בכוירים [בכורים] (די ערשט־געבויערענע פֿון
ציגן און שעפּסן).

אָבער ווי צו מענטשן, וועלכע וואנען צו בלייבן אויפן גאס צו קוקן, ווי
גאט, דאס פֿייער, וועט אראפפֿייניג עסן זיינע קארבאנעס [קרבנות]! די מענטשן
האבן אין דער נאכט פון פייסעך [פּסח] פון שרעק זיך באהאלטן אין זייערע
געצעלטן. די שוועלן און פֿירטעלקעס פֿון זייערע טירן פֿלעגן זיי באשפּריצן
מיט בלוט, ווייל זיי פֿלעגן גלויבן, אז דאס איז די בעסטע טרופֿע [תּרופֿה], אז
דער שרעקלעכער גאט זאל זיך אין דער נאכט ניט אריינרייסן אין געצעלט און
פֿארניכטן די מענטשן.

אַזוי האט דער געצנדינערישער [געצן־דינערישער] וואנדער־שייוועט
[שבֿט] איסראעל [ישׂראל] געפֿייערט זיין פֿרילינג־יאנטעוו [יום־טובֿ]—פֿייסעך
[פּסח]. אזוי האט ער קארבאנעס [קרבנות] געבראכט זיין גאט יעהאָווע (יהוה),
וועלכער האט געוואוינט אויפֿן בארג סינאַי.

Nokh itster gefinen zikh eynike vanderndike Arabishe shvotim, velkhe fayern oyf aza oyfn zeyer friling-yontev, brengen zey er got a korbn di pkhoyrim fun shepsn un tsign.

Shpeter, ven di Yidn zaynen in land Kenaan ibergegangen shoyn tsu erd-arbet, hobn zey ongehoybn dinen zeyer Got oyf a nayem shteyger. Khuts shepsn un tsign flegn zey nokh mekhabed zayn im mit di frukhtn fun der erd, velkhe zey hobn baarbet. **In dem sheynem friling-yontev, ven dort flegt ersht fartik vern di tvue, flegn zey oyf gikh oysbakn kikhlekh un mekhabed zayn dermit zeyer Got.**

Un nokh shpeter, ven di koyhanim hobn bazetst dem Yidishn Got in Beys-Hamikdesh un hobn im dort korbones gebrakht, hobn zey dem friling-yontev farvandlt in a yontev, vos derhoybt zeyer Got als vundershafer un bafrayer. **Der getsndinerisher korbn fun ershtgeboyrene shepsn iz gevorn a korbn-Peysekh. Dos oyf gikh oysgebakene kikhl, mit velkhn di getsndiner hobn mekhabed geven zeyer Got, iz in matse farvandlt gevorn.**

Gor poshet hot di farvandlung nit gekont forkumen. **S'iz noytik geven a legende, a sheyne, a tsutsiendike, velkhe zol dem Got derhoybn un zayne mitsves heylikn.**

Hot zikh geshafn di legende fun Yetsies-Mitsraim.

Di koyhanim hobn nit in gantsn oysgetrakht di dozike legende.

נאָך איצטער געפֿינען זיך איייניקע וואַנדערנדיקע אַראַבישע שוואַטים [שבטים], וועלכע פֿירן אויף אזא אויפֿן זייער פֿרילינג־יאָנטעוו, ברענגען זיי ער גאָט אַ קאָרבן [קרבן] די בכורים [בכורים] פֿון שעפּסן און ציגן.

שפּעטער, ווען די ייִדן זיינען אין לאַנד כּנענן [כנען] איבערגעגאַנגען שיין צו ערד־אַרבעט, האָבן זיי אָנגעהויבן דינען זייער גאָט אויף אַ נייעם שטייגער. בוץ שעפּסן און ציגן פֿלעגן זיי נאָך מעכּאַבעד [מכבד] זיין אים מיט די פֿרוכטן פֿון דער ערד, וועלכע זיי האָבן באַאַרבעט. אין דעם שיינעם פֿרילינג־יאָנטעוו [יום־טוב], ווען דאָרט פֿלעגט ערשט פֿאַרטיק ווערן די טוווע די תּבֿואה], פֿלעגן זיי אויף גיך אויסבאַקן קויקלעך און מעכּאַבעד [מכבד] זיין דערמיט זייער גאָט.

און נאָך שפּעטער, ווען די כּוהאַנים [כהנים] האָבן באַזעצט דעם ייִדישן גאָט אין בייס־האַמיקדעש [בית־המיקדש] און האָבן אים דאָרט קאָרבאַנעס [קרבנות] געבראַכט, האָבן זיי דעם פֿרילינג־יאָנטעוו [יום־טוב] פֿאַרוואַנדלט אין אַ יאָנטעוו [יום־טוב], וואָס דערהויבט זייער גאָט אַלס וווּנדערשאַפֿער און באַפֿרייער. דער געגנדינערישער [געגן־דינערישער] קאָרבן [קרבן] פֿון ערשט־געבוירענע שעפּסן איז געוואָרן אַ קאָרבן־פּייסעך [קרבן פּסח]. דאָס אויף גיך אויסגעבאַקענע קויקל, מיט וועלכן די געגנדינער [געגן־דינער] האָבן מעכּאַבעד [מכבד] געווען זייער גאָט, איז אין מאַצע [מצה] פֿאַרוואַנדלט געוואָרן.

גאָר פּאַשעט [פשוט] האָט די פֿאַרוואַנדלונג ניט געקאָנט פֿאָרקומען. ס'איז נייטיק געוואָרן אַ לעגענדע, אַ שיינע, אַ צוציענדיקע, וועלכע זאָל דעם גאָט דערהויבן און זיינע מיצוועס [מיצוות] הייליקן.

האָט זיך געשאַפֿן די לעגענדע פֿון יעציעס־מיצראַיִם [יציאת־מצרים].

די כּוהאַנים [כהנים] האָבן ניט אין גאַנצן אויסגעטראַכט די דאָזיקע

Ba di Yidn zaynen geven nit veynik alte mayses, vos hobn geshtamt fun der tsayt, ven di farsheydene shvotim fun velkhe es iz oysgevaksn dernokh dos Yidishe folk, hobn gefirt a vander-lebn, flegn arayndringen in farsheydene lender, kemfn mit farsheydene felker. **Di koyhanim hobn di farsheydene legendes "baarbet" un "tsugepast" tsu zeyere tsiln.** Dem hoyptheld fun di mayses hobn zey gemakht dem Got, velkhn zey dinen.

Fun farsheydene ekn fun land, fun di vaytste vinklekh flegn kumen fusgeyer tsum heylikn templ—tsum Beys-Hamikdesh mit zeyere korbones. A sakh arbet iz demolt geven far Gots diner—far di koyhanim, un zey flegn derbay gor nit shlekht fardinen.

Vos vayter me hot zikh opgerukt in tsayt fun dem emesn urshprung fun di korbones un der matse, fun dem uraltn getsndinerishn friling-yontev, alts mer hot di koyhanim-kaste tsugegebn naye mayses un vunder tsum yontev, alts naye dinim far im tsugetrakht un hobn im oyf lang farfestikt als dem grestn yontev fun natsyonaln Got.

In der gantser oysgetrakhter mayse fun Yetsies-Mitsraim gefint ir nit keyn eyn vort vegn dem, az dos folk aleyn zol oyfshteyn kegn zayne unterdriker, az dos folk aleyn zol khotsh protestirn kegn knekhtshaft. Dos folk hot nor gekrekhtset, un Got hot gehert zayne geshrayen. Der hoyptheld fun der legende iz nit dos folk, nor Got—der Got fun vunder un kuntsn, a Got fun tsorn—far di, vos dinen im nit, un fun rakhmones—far di, velkhe

לעגנענדע. בא די יידן זײנען געווען ניט ווייניק אַלטע מײסעס [מעשיות], וואָס האָבן געשטאַמט פֿון דער צייט, ווען די פֿאַרשײדענע שװאָטים [שבטים] פֿון וועלכע עס איז אויסגעוואַקסן דערנאָך דאָס ײדישע פֿאָלק, האָבן געפֿירט אַ וואַנדער-לעבן, פֿלעגן אַרײנדרינגען אין פֿאַרשײדענע לענדער, קעמפֿן מיט פֿאַרשײדענע פֿעלקער. די קויהאַנים [כהנים] האָבן די פֿאַרשײדענע לעגענדעס "באַאַרבעט" און "צוגעפּאַסט" צו זײערע ציל. דעם הויפּטהעלד פֿון די מײסעס [מעשיות] האָבן זיי געמאַכט דעם גאָט, וועלכן זיי דינען.

פֿון פֿאַרשײדענע עקן פֿון לאַנד, פֿון די ווייטסטע ווינקלעך פֿלעגן קומען פּוסגײער צום הייליקן טעמפּל–צום בייס-האַמיקדש [בית-המיקדש] מיט זײערע קאָרבאָנעס [קרבנות]. אַ סאַך [סך] אַרבעט איז דעמאָלט געווען פֿאַר גאָטס דינער–פֿאַר די קויהאַנים [כהנים], און זיי פֿלעגן דערבײ גאָר ניט שלעכט פֿאַרדינען.

וואָס ווייטער מע האָט זיך אָפּגערוקט אין צייט פֿון דעם עמעס [אמת] אורשפּרונג פֿון די קאָרבאָנעס [קרבנות] און דער מאַצע [מצה], פֿון דעם אוראַלטן געעצנדינערישן [געצן-דינערישן] פֿרילינג-יאַנטעוו [יום-טוב], אַלץ מער האָט די קויהאַנים-קאַסטע [כהנים] צוגעגעבן נייע מײסעס [מעשיות] און וווּנדער צום יאַנטעוו [יום-טוב], אַלץ נייע דינים פֿאַר אים צוגעטראַכט און האָבן אים אויף לאַנג פֿאַרפֿעסטיקט אַלס דעם גרעסטן יאַנטעוו [יום-טוב] פֿון נאַציאָנאַלן גאָט.

אין דער גאַנצער אויסגעטראַכטער מײסע [מעשה] פֿון יעציעס-מיצראַים [יציאת-מצרים] געפֿינט איר ניט קיין איין וואָרט וועגן דעם, אַז דאָס פֿאָלק אַליין זאָל אויפֿשטיין קעגן זײנע אונטערדריקער, אַז דאָס פֿאָלק אַליין זאָל באַטש פראָטעסטירן קעגן קנעכטשאַפֿט. דאָס פֿאָלק האָט נאָר געקרעכצעט, און גאָט האָט געהערט זײנע געשרייען. דער הויפּטהעלד פֿון דער לעגענדע איז ניט דאָס פֿאָלק, נאָר גאָט–דער גאָט פֿון וווּנדער און קונצן, אַ גאָט פֿון צאָרן–פֿאַר די, וואָס דינען אים ניט, און פֿון ראַכמאָנעס [רחמנות]–פֿאַר די, וועלכע זיינען אים

zaynen im untertenik. A Got, vos kon mit a mol onshikn layz on a shir, zhabes on a tsol, krets oyfn gantsn layb, blut oyfn gantsn land. Er kon hargenen ale pkhoyrim, kon fun a shtekn makhn a shlang, kon mit eyn mol trukn makhn dem yam, shit fun himl man, vos hot a tam, velkhn ir vilt: fun fleysh, fun fish, kez, puter, tsholnt. Iz dos nit keyn groyser Got? Kon men far im nit moyre hobn? Darf men im, aza tayern Got, nit libn? Iz er nit vert, az me zol im brengen korbones?

Der Beys-Hamikdesh iz khorev gevorn, di korbones—botl gevorn. Gots diner zaynen ober geblibn, zey zorgn, az der gloybn fun folk zol kholile nit shvakher vern, az di hakhnoses far Gots dinst zoln nit klener vern. Korbones vern farbitn mit tfiles, s'vaksn di tsol mitsves, velkhe yeder Yid muz oysfiln kegn Got, semern zikh di aveyres, mit velkhe me kon Got dertsorenen, un a gantser hogl fun dinim shitn zikh oyf di Yidishe kep, dinim vos me meg ton un vos me tor nit ton; dinim vegn dem, vos Got vil, az me zol ton in der fri, un vos ba nakht; vos far a tfile darf men zogn bam oyfshteyn, un vos far a tfile bam leygn zikh shlofn; vos far a brokhe farn esn, un vosere nokhn esn; vos far a brokhe oyf broyt, un velkhe oyf vaser; vi loybt men Got far kartofl, un vi far epl; vi far hirzhene kashe, un vi far knishes; vos far a komplimentn makht men Got derfar, vos er hot gemakht a mogn bam mentshn, un vi zol men im loybn derfar, vos er makht a regn-boygn. Me darf hobn Gots brokhe oyf khasene hobn, on zayn derloybenish tor men zikh nit getn. Nor ba zayn heyliker Toyre kon men dos kind a nomen gebn, un nokh zayn gebot nokh darf men dos kind mal zayn; tsulib im darf men pidyen-haben makhn, im darf men zogn haleluyo; zayn heylikn nomen iz gevidmet asher-yotser; er vil nit, az me zol far zeks sho esn milkhiks nokh fleyshiks; er kon dos nit fartrogn, ven me farbayt a fleyshike lefl oyf a milkhike; er vil, az me zol

אונטערטעניק, אַ גאָט, וואָס קאָן מיט אַ מאָל אָנשיקן לייז אָן אַ שיר [שיעור], זשאַבעס אָן אַ צאָל, קרעץ אויפֿן גאַנצן לייב, בלוט אויפֿן גאַנצן לאַנד. ער קאָן האַרגענען [הרגענען] אַלע בכוירים [בכורים], קאָן פֿון אַ שטעטק מאַכן אַ שלאַנג, קאָן מיט אַ מאָל טרוקן מאַכן דעם יאַם [ים], שיט פֿון הימל מאַן, וואָס האָט אַ טאַם, וועלכן איר ווילט: פֿון פֿלייש, פֿון פֿיש, קעז, פּוטער, טשאָלנט. איז דאָס ניט קיין גרויסער גאָט? קאָן מען פֿאַר אים ניט מוירע [מורא] האָבן? דאַרף מען אים, אַזאַ טייערן גאָט, ניט ליבן? איז ער ניט ווערט, אַז מע זאָל אים ברענגען קאָרבאָנעס [קרבנות]?

דער בייס-האַמיקדעש [בית-המיקדש] איז באַראַוו [חרוב] געוואָרן, די קאָרבאָנעס [קרבנות]—באַטל [בטל] געוואָרן. גאָטס דינער זיינען אָבער געבליבן, זיי זאָרגן, אַז דער גלויבן פֿון פֿאָלק זאָל באַלילע [חלילה] ניט שוואַבער ווערן, אַז די האַבנאַסעס [הכנסות] פֿאַר גאָטס דינסט זאָלן ניט קלענער ווערן. קאָרבאָנעס [קרבנות] ווערן פֿאַרביטן מיט טפֿילעס [תפילות], ס'וואַקסן די צאָל מיצוועס [מיצוות], וועלכע יעדער ייד מוז אויספֿילן קעגן גאָט, סעמערן זיך די אַווייִרעס, מיט וועלכע מע קאָן גאָט דערצאָרענען, און אַ גאַנצער האַגל פֿון דינים שיטן זיך אויף די יידישע קעפּ, דינים וואָס מע מעג מאַן און וואָס מע טאָר ניט טאָן; דינים וועגן דעם, וואָס גאָט וויל, אַז מען זאָל טאָן אין דער פֿרי, און וואָס בא נאַכט; וואָס פֿאַר אַ טפֿילע [תפילה] דאַרף מען זאָגן באַם אויפֿשטיין, און וואָס פֿאַר אַ טפֿילע [תפילה] באַם לייגן זיך שלאָפֿן; וואָס פֿאַר אַ בראָכע [ברכה] פֿאַרן עסן, און וואַסערע נאָכן עסן; וואָס פֿאַר אַ בראָכע [ברכה] אויף ברויט, און וועלכע אויף וואַסער; ווי לויבט מען גאָט פֿאַר קאַרטאָפֿל, און ווי פֿאַר עפּל; ווי פֿאַר הירזשענע קאַשע, און ווי פֿאַר קנישעס; וואָס פֿאַר אַ קאָמפּלימענטן מאַכט מען גאָט דערפֿאַר, וואָס ער האָט געמאַכט אַ מאָן באַם מענטשן, און ווי זאָל מען אים לויבן דערפֿאַר, וואָס ער מאַכט אַ רעגן־בויגן. מע דאַרף האָבן גאָטס בראָכע אויף באַסענע כּאַסענע [חתונה] האָבן, אָן זיין דערלויבעניש טאָר מען זיך ניט גאָט געטן. נאָר באַ זיין הייליקער טוירע [תורה] קאָן מען דאָס קינד אַ נאָמען געבן, און נאָך זיין געבאָט מען נאָך דאַרף מען דאָס קינד מאָל [מל] זיין; צוליב אים דאַרף מען פּידיון־האַבען [פדיון-הבן] מאַכן, אים דאַרף מען זאָגן האַלעלויאַ [הללויה]; זיין הייליקן נאָמען איז געוווידמעט אַשער־יאָצער; ער וויל

ophitn Peysekh nokh ale dinim, s'zol kholile keyn brekl khomets in a Yidisher shtub nit zayn.

Dinim on shir un on a tsol, mitsves nit tsu tseyln. Aveyres nit ibertsurekhenen.

Un far a kleynink aveyrele shtroft oft Got, vi far a groyser. Kedey tsu rateven Gots folk fun shtrof far zind, vos yeder mentsh kon ton, bavustzinik oder nit bavustzinik, zorgn far im di kley-koydesh, Gots diner: rabonim, shokhtim, dayonim, velkhe veysn pinktlekh Gots dinim. Veysn—vos Got derloybt un vos er farbot. Zey lernen dos folk Gots Toyre, zey derklern yeder os fun der heyliker Toyre, zey paskenen shayles, vos treyf iz un vos kosher, vos me meg ton un vos me tor nit, zey zaynen mesader kedushn unter der khupe un shraybn di tsvelf shures ba get. Zorgn far di lebedike un zeen, az zey zoln hobn a koshere mikve. Zey daygen far di toyte un farzorgn zey mit a khevre-kedishe, mit kadesh, mit likht, mit yortsayt. On a rov un a shoykhet iz gor dos lebn keyn lebn nit, vayl on zey kon men kholile opton azelkhe maysim, az Got vet dos keyn mol nit moykhl zayn: s'iz rekht, az me zol bentshn mit an esreg on a pitem, me zol lib hobn a meydl on a brokhe, me zol gor, nit for keyn Yidn gedakht, a posele mezuze hobn bam tir.

Haynt Peysekh! Peysekh on dem rov un on dem shoykhet kon

ניט, אַז מע זאָל פֿאַר זעקס שאַ עסן מילביקס נאָך פֿלײשיקס; ער קאָן ניט דאָס ניט פֿאַרטראָגן, וװען מע פֿאַרבײַט אַ פֿלײשיקע לעפֿל אױף אַ מילביקע; ער װיל, אַז מע זאָל אָפּהיטן פּײסעך [פסח] נאָך אַלע דינים, ס׳זאָל באַלילע [חלילה] קײן ברעקל באָמעץ [חמץ] אין אַ ייִדישער שטוב ניט זײַן.

דינים אַן שיר [שיעור] און אַן אַ צאָל, מיצװעס [מיצװת] ניט צו צײלן. אַװײרעס [עבירות] ניט איבערצורעכענען.

און פֿאַר אַ קלײנינק אַװײרעלע [עבירהלע] שטראָפֿט אָפֿט גאָט, װי פֿאַר אַ גרױסער. קעדײַ [כדי] צו ראַטעװען גאָטס פֿאָלק פֿון שטראָף פֿאַר זינד, װאָס יעדער מענטש קאָן טאָן, באַװוּסטזיניק אָדער ניט באַװוּסטזיניק, זאָרגן פֿאַר אים די קליי־קױדעשס [כלי־קודש], גאָטס דינער: ראַבאָנים [רבנים], שאָכטים [שוחטים], דיאָנים [דיינים], װעלכע װײַסן פֿינקטלעך גאָטס דינים. װײַסן–– װאָס גאָט דערלױבט און װאָס ער פֿאַרבאָט. זײ לערנען דאָס פֿאָלק גאָטס טײַרע [תּורה], זײ דערקלערן יעדער אָס [אות] פֿון דער הײליקער טײַרע [תּורה], זײ פּאַסקענען [פּסקענען] שײלעס [שאלות], װאָס טרײף איז און װאָס קאָשער, װאָס מע מעג טאָן און װאָס מע טאָר ניט, זײ זײַנען מעסאַדער [מסדר] קעדישן [קידושין] אונטער דער כופּע [חופּה] און שרײַבן די צװעלף שורעס [שורות] באַ געט [גט]. זאָרגן פֿאַר די לעבעדיקע און טױע, אַז זײ זאָלן האָבן אַ קאָשערע [כּשרע] מיקװע [מיקוה]. זײ דײגען [דאגהן] פֿאַר די טױטע און פֿאַרזאָרגן זײ מיט אַ בעװוּרע־קעװוּרישע [חברה־קדישא], מיט קאָדעש [קדיש], מיט ליבט, מיט יאָרצײַט. אָן אַ ראָװ [רב] און אַ שױבעט [שוחט] איז גאָר דאָס לעבן קײן לעבן ניט, װײַל אָן זײ קאָן מען באַלילע [חלילה] אָפּטאָן אַזעלכע מײַסים [מעשׂים], אַז גאָט װעט דאָס קײן מאָל ניט מױכל [מוחל] זײַן: ס׳איז רעכט, אַז מע זאָל בענטשן מיט אַן עסרעג [אתרוג] אָן אַ פּיטעם [פּיטום], מע זאָל ליב האָבן אַ מײדל אָן אַ בראָכע [ברכה], מע זאָל גאָר, ניט פֿאַר קײן ייִדן געדאַכט, אַ פֿאַסעלע [פּסולע] מעזוזע [מזוזה] האָבן באַם טיר.

הײַנט פּײסעך [פסח]! פּײסעך [פסח] אָן דעם ראָװ [רב] און אָן דעם

men take dokh nit oyskumen! Vi vet ir oyskumen on a rov, ven ir vet gefinen a gershtn in gekekhts? Un vos vet ir take ton, az a khometsdike goye vet zikh onrirn on der Peysekhdiker deyzhke burikes, un ba vemen vet ir "farkoyfn" ayer khomets, ver vet aykh bazorgn mit kharoyses, mit shmure-matse, un ver vet aykh derklern, vi tsu kashern ayere fanen un lefl? Alts der rov!

Der getsndinerisher korbn dem kaasdikn got oyf dem fayershpayendikn Barg Sinai, dos frishinke kikhl, vos di getsndiner—erdarbeter flegn brengen in friling a matone zeyer got, iz mit der hilf fun di rabonim, khakhomim sof-kol-sof gevorn a yontev, ven keyn brekl broyt tor zikh in shtub nit gefinen, ven di keylim, vos me nitst a gants yor, darfn oyfn beydem aroyfgetrogn vern, ven alts, vos ir hot tsugegreyt esn a gants yor, tort ir nit gebroykhn, ayer gantsn khomets muzt ir farbrenen.

Shtark iberboygn dem shtekn iz ober geferlekh. Di rabonim farshteyen, az a bafel tsu farbrenen dem gantsn khomets vet fun zeyer praktisher kehile nit oysgefirt vern. A tsu tayere mitsve far zey! Un beemes, ver vet fun aza mayse fardinen? Di rabonim faln ober oyf a getlekhn aynfal. Anshtot dem khomets tsu farbrenen, gibn zey an eytse im oyf der tsayt fun Peysekh tsu farkoyfn a goy. Di gantse eyde Yidn farkoyfn yederer bazunder dem khomets dem rov, oder dem shoykhet (azoy oyf tsu kloymersht), un zey farkoyfn shoyn dem khomets dem bod-goy. Tsu der origineler komertsyeler operatsye leygt der rov un der shoykhet gor veynik tsu. Zey fardinen a sakh mer eyder der bod-goy, velkher vert arayngetsoygn far a por gildn in dem

שויכעט [שוחט] קאָן מען טאַקע דאָך ניט אויסקומען! ווי וועט איר אויסקומען
אָן אַ רצוו [רב], ווען איר וועט געפֿינען אַ גערשטן אין געקעכטס? און וואָס
וועט איר טאַקע טאָן, אַז אַ באַמעצדיקע [חמצדיקע] גריע וועט זיך אַנירדן אן
דער פּייסעאַבעדיקער [פּסחאדיקער] דייזשקע בורדיקעס, און בא ווימעמען וועט איר
„פֿאַרקויפֿן" אייער כאַמעץ [חמץ], ווער וועט אייך באַזאָרגן מיט באַרייסעס
[חרוסת], מיט שמורע־מאַצע [שמורה־מצה], און ווער וועט אייך דערקלערן, ווי
צו קאַשערן [כשרן] אייערע פֿאַנצען און לעפֿל? אַלץ דער רצוו [רב]!

דער געצנדינערישער [געצן־דינערישער] קאָרבן [קרבן] דעם קאָעסדיקן
[קאָעסדיקן] גאָט אויף דעם פֿיערשפּייענדיקן באַרג סינאַי, דאָס פֿרישינקע קיבל,
וואָס די געצנדינער [געצן־דינער]—ערדאַרבעטער פֿלעגן ברענגען אין פֿרילינג
אַ מאָטאַנע זייער גאָט, איז מיט דער הילף פֿון די ראַבאָניס [רבנים], כאַכאַמים
[חכמים] סאָף־קאָל־סאָף [סוף־כּל־סוף] געוואָרן אַ יאַנטעוו, ווען קיין בערעקל
ברויט מאַר זיך אין שטוב ניט געפֿינען, ווען די קיילים [כּלים], וואָס מע ניצט
אַ גאַנץ יאָר, דאַרפֿן אויפֿן ביידעם אַריופֿגעטראָגן ווערן, ווען אַלץ, וואָס איר
האָט צוגעגריט עסן אַ גאַנץ יאָר, טאָרט איר ניט געברויכן, אייער גאַנצן כאַמעץ
[חמץ] מוזט איר פֿאַרברענען.

שטאַרק איבערבייזון דעם שטעקן איז אָבער געפֿערלעך. די ראַבאָניס
[רבנים] פֿאַרשטייען, אַז אַ באַפֿעל צו פֿאַרברענען דעם גאַנצן כאַמעץ [חמץ]
ווער פֿון זייער פּראַקטישער קעהילע [קהילה] ניט אויסגעפֿירט ווערן. אַ צו
טייערע מיצוה [מצוה] פֿאַר זיי! און בעשעמעס [באמת], ווער וועט פֿון אַזאַ
מיאסע [מעשה] פֿאַרדינען? די ראַבאָניס [רבנים] פֿאַלן אָבער אויף אַ געטלעכן
איינפֿאַל. אַנשטאָט דעם כאַמעץ [חמץ] צו פֿאַרברענען, גיבן זיי אַן אייצע
[עצה] אים אויף דער צייט פֿון פֿייסעך [פּסח] צו פֿאַרקויפֿן אַ גוי. די גאַנצע
איידע יידן פֿאַרקויפֿן יעדערער באַזונדער דעם כאַמעץ [חמץ] דעם רצוו
[רב], אָדער דעם שויכעט [שוחט] (אַזוי אויף צו קליימערשט [כּלומרשט]), און
זיי פֿאַרקויפֿן שוין דעם כאַמעץ [חמץ] דעם באַד־גוי. צו דער אָריגינעלער
קאָמערציעלער אָפּעראַציע לייגט דער רצוו [רב] און דער שויכעט [שוחט] גאָר

shutfesdikn kunts optsunarn Got.

Ober khomets farbrenen iz a mitsve, un zi vert oykh oysgefirt. Mit a hiltserner lefl in eyn hant un mit a feder fun a hun in der anderer zukht der frumer Yid in ale vinkelekh di shtiklekh broyt, vos er aleyn hot mit etlekhe minut frier avekgeleygt, gefint zey, farshteyt zikh. Klaybt zey pinktlekh tsunoyf in der hiltserner lefl, makht derbay a brokhe, loybt dem Reboyne-shel-oylem, un oyf morgn farbrent er di lefl mit di breklekh in oyvn, makht, farshteyt zikh, vider a brokhe, un loybt nokh a mol Got, vos er hot zayn folk Yisroel gegebn aza sheyne mitsve, vi byer khomets.

Di ale mitsves mit zeyere protsedures zaynen pinktlekh fargeshribn in di heylike sforim. Far zeyer oysfirn vert tsugezogt oylem-habe, far zeyer nit oysfirn—di greste shtrofn fun groysn Yidishn Got.

Der gloybn in Got zol nit opgeshvakht vern, di vunder zayne zoln kholile nit fargesn vern, muzn zey fun yor tsu yor vider dertseylt vern in ale zeyere eyntslheytn ba a fayerlekh-gemakhter shtimung, mit farsheydene tseremonyes, mit simbolishe remozim.

Yeder zakh hot zayn bashtimt ort: der morer, di kharoyses, di zroye, di karpes,—Got zol aykh hitn avektsuleygn di zroye dort, vu es iz fargeshribn tsu leygn di kharoyses! Un esn zolt ir ongeleyenterheyt,

וייניק צו. זיי פֿאַרדינען אַ סאַך [סך] מער איידער דער באַד-גוי, וועלכער ווערט אַרײַנגעצויגן פֿאַר אַ פֿאָר גילדן אין דעם שותּפֿעסדיקן [שותּפֿותדיקן] קוניץ אָפּצונאַרן גאָט.

אָבער באַמעץ [חמץ] פֿאַרברענען איז אַ מיצווע [מיצווה], און זי ווערט אויך אויסגעפֿירט. מיט אַ הילצערנער לעפֿל אין איין האַנט און מיט אַ פֿעדער פֿון אַ הון אין דער אַנדערער זוכט דער פֿרומער ייִד אין אַלע ווינקעלעך די שטיקלעך ברויט, וואָס ער אַליין האָט מיט עטלעכע מינוט פֿריִער אַוועקגעלייגט, געפֿינט זיי, פֿאַרשטייט זיך. קלייבט זיי פֿינקטלעך צונויף אין דער הילצערנער לעפֿל, מאַכט דערבײַ אַ בראָכע [ברכה], לויבט דעם רעבוינע-שעל-אוילעם [רבונו-של-עולם], און אויף מאָרגן פֿאַרברענט ער די לעפֿל מיט די ברעקלעך אין אַן אויוון, מאַכט, פֿאַרשטייט זיך, ווידער אַ בראָכע [ברכה], און לויבט נאָך אַ מאָל גאָט, וואָס ער האָט זײַן פֿאָלק איסראַעל געגעבן אַזאַ שיינע מיצווע [מיצווה], ווי ביער באַמעץ [ביעור־חמץ].

די אַלע מיצוועס [מיצוות] מיט זייערע פּראָצעדורעס זײַנען פֿינקטלעך פֿאַרגעשריבן אין די הייליקע ספֿאָרים [ספֿרים]. פֿאַר זייער אויספֿירן ווערט צוגעזאָגט אוילעם-האַבע [עולם-הבא], פֿאַר זייער ניט אויספֿירן—די גרעסטע שטראָפֿן פֿון גרויסן ייִדישן גאָט.

דער גלויבן אין גאָט זאָל ניט אָפּגעשוואַכט ווערן, די ווונדער זײַנע זאָלן באַלילע [חלילה] ניט פֿאַרגעסן ווערן, מוזן זיי פֿון יאָר צו יאָר ווידער דערצײַלט ווערן אין אַלע זייערע אייניצלהייטן בײַ אַ פֿײַערלעך-געמאַכטער שטימונג, מיט פֿאַרשיידענע צערעמאָניעס, מיט סימבאָלישע רעמאָזים [רמזים].

יעדער זאַך האָט זײַן באַשטימט אָרט: דער מאָרער [מרור], די באַרויסעם [חרוסת], די זרויע [זרוע], די קאָרפּעס [כרפּס],—גאָט זאָל אײַך היטן אַוועקצולייגן די זרויע [זרוע] דאָרט, וווּ עס איז פֿאַרגעשריבן צו לייגן די

hoybt oyf dem kos, ven s'iz ongevizn in der Hagode, est dem morer, punkt azoy vi Hilel hot im gegesn, ven der Beys-Hamikdesh iz nokh geven. Tut alts, vi Got hot geheysn. Got iz a groyser, a shtarker, a vunder-makher! Ot zog nokh a mol di Hagode, vestu zeen vos far a Got du host!

Gloyb in dayn Got, gloyb in zayne vunder, gloyb in zayn groyskeyt. Vestu nit gloybn, vestu zayn vunder nit dertseyln—bistu a roshe! Un veystu vos di Hagode heyst ton mit a roshe, vos gloybt nit in Gots vunder?—Hak im oys di tseyner, dem roshe, vayl er gloybt nit in Hakodesh Borekh Hu, un zog im, az ven azelkhe reshoim, vi er, voltn in Mitsraim geven, volt zey Got fun dort nit oysgeleyzt. Got hot lib nor di, vos gloybn in zayn koyekh un loybn zayn libn nomen.

Nor Got aleyn kon bafrayen, nor er perzenlekh, durkh zayne groyse vunder—azoy vert ibergekhazert on a shir mol in der Hagode.

Vifl tseyner voltn dos di rabonim darfn oysbrekhn (ven mevolt zey nor gelozn!) di reshoim, apikorsim, velkhe zingen in zeyer revolut-syonerer lid: "un keyner vet unz nit bafrayen, nit got aleyn un nit keyn held, mit unzer eygenem kley-zayen bafrayen veln mir di velt!"

Got hot zayn hoyz, Got rut in Tsyen, ahin hot er tsugezogt tsu brengen zayn folk Yisroel, ven dos folk vet dos ba im nor fardinen.

באַריסעם [חרוסת]! און עסן זאָלט איר אָנגעלייענטערהייט, הויבט אויף דעם קאָס [כּוס], ווען ס׳איז אָנגעוויזן אין דער האַגאַדע [הגדה], עסט דעם מאָרער [מרור], פּונקט אַזוי ווי הילעל האָט אים געגעסן, ווען דער בייס־האַמיקדעש [בית־המקדש] איז נאָך געווען. טוט אַלץ, ווי גאָט האָט געהייסן. גאָט איז אַ גרויסער, אַ שטאַרקער, אַ וווּנדער־מאַכער! אָט זאָג נאָך אַ מאָל די האַגאַדע [הגדה], ווערסטו זען וואָס פֿאַר אַ גאָט דו האָסט!

גלויב אין דיין גאָט, גלויב אין זיינע וווּנדער, גלויב אין זיין גרויסקייט. ווייסטו ניט גלויבן, ווערסטו זיין וווּנדער ניט דערציילן—ביסטו אַ רשעא [רשע]! און ווייסטו וואָס די האַגאַדע [הגדה] הייסט טאָן מיט אַ רשעא [רשע], וואָס גלויבט ניט אין גאָטס וווּנדער?—האַק אים אויס די ציינער, דעם רשעא [רשע], ווייל ער גלויבט ניט אין דעם האַקאָדעש באָרעך הו [הקדוש ברוך הוא], און זאָג אים, אַז ווען אַזעלבע רעשאים [רשעים], ווי ער, וואָלטן אין מיצראַים [מצרים] געווען, וואָלט זיי גאָט פֿון דאָרט ניט אויסגעלייזט. גאָט האָט ליב נאָר די, וואָס גלויבן אין זיין קוֹיעך [כּוח] און לויבן זיין ליבן נאָמען.

נאָר גאָט אַליין קאָן באַפֿרייען, נאָר ער פֿערזוענלעך, דורך זיינע גרויסע וווּנדער—אַזוי ווערט איבערגעבאַזערט [איבערגעחזרט] אַן אַשיר [שיעור] מאָל אין דער האַגאַדע [הגדה].

וויפֿל ציינער וואָלטן דאָס די ראַבאַנים [רבנים] דאַרפֿן אויסברעכן (ווען מעוואַלט זיי נאָר געלאָזן!) די רעשאַים [רשעים], אַפּיקאָרסים [אפיקורסים], וועלכע זינגען אין זייער רעוואָלוציאָנערער ליד: ״און קיינער וועט אונז ניט באַפֿרייען, ניט גאָט אַליין און ניט קיין העלד, מיט אונזער אייגענעם קליי־זייען [כּלי־זיין] באַפֿרייען וועלן מיר די וועלט!״

גאָט האָט זיין הויז, גאָט רוט אין ציען [ציון], אַהין האָט ער צוגעזאָגט צו ברענגען זיין פֿאָלק איסראַעל [ישראל], ווען דאָס פֿאָלק וועט דאָס בא

Un di Hagode-zoger, nokh dem, vi zey hobn dertseylt ale vunder fun Got, vos er hot gemakht ba Yetsies-Mitsraim, nokh dem, vi zey hobn im derfar geloybt un gedankt, nokh ale komplimentn, vos zey hobn gemakht in di haleluyos zeyer groysn, sheynem, klugn, raykhn, gutn Got,—nokh alem dem betn zey im, er zol zey bashern tsu derlebn di groyse simkhe, ven zey veln vider zayn in Yerusholaim, veln dort brengen korbones un veln shpritsn dos blut fun di gekoylete shepsn oyf di vent fun dem heylikn mizbeyekh.

In tsvantsikstn yorhundert, in der tsayt fun luftshifn un radyo, in der epokhe fun sotsyalistishe revolutsyes—betn frume Yidn, Got zol zey baglikn, az zey zoln vider konen brengen korbones!

Durkh oysgetrakhte mayses fun Yetsies-Mitsraim, durkh dertseylungen fun ibernatirlekhe vunder, in velkhe keyn eyn gebildeter mentsh kon nit gloybn, vayl er veyst di gezetsn fun der natur un di derklerung fun ire dershaynungen, durkh farsheydene tseremonyes, dinim, brokhes un tfiles zukht di klerikale kaste ayntsuhaltn dem gloybn in natsyonaln Got.

Tsuzamen mit der libe un moyre far dem Got fun Yisroel flantsn zey sine un has tsu ale andere felker, velkhe gloybn nit in YHWH, un dinen andere geter. Ven me efnt di tir in mitn oprikhtn dem seyder oyf arayntsulozn Eleyohu-Hanovi, far velkhn s'iz tsugegreyt a bazunder bekher vayn, betn di Hagode-zoger zeyer Got, er zol oysgisn zayn kas oyf di felker, vos dinen im nit un zol zey in gantsn farnikhtn fun der erd.

אים נאָר פֿאַרדינען. און די האַגאַדע־זאָגער [הגדה]. נאָך דעם, ווי זיי האָבן דערצייַלט אַלע וווּנדער פֿון גאָט, וואָס ער האָט געמאַכט בייַ יעציעס־מיצראים [יציאת־מצרים], נאָך דעם, ווי זיי האָבן אים דערפֿאַר געלויבט און געדאַנקט, נאָך אַלע קאָמפּלימענטן, וואָס זיי האָבן געמאַכט אין די הַאלעלויעס [הלליות] זייער גרויסן, שיינעם, קלוגן, רייכן, גוטן גאָט,—נאָך אַלע דעם בעטן זיי אים, ער זאָל זיי באַשערן צו דערלעבן די גרויסע סימכע [שמחה], ווען זיי וועלן ווידער זיין אין יערושאַלאַים [ירושלים], וועלן דאָרט ברענגען קאָרבאַנעס [קרבנות] און וועלן שפּריצן דאָס בלוט פֿון די געקוילעטע שעפּסן אויף די ווענט פֿון דעם הייליקן מיזביעך [מזבח].

אין צוואַנציקסטן יאָרהונדערט, אין דער צייט פֿון לופֿטשיפֿן און ראַדיאָ, אין דער עפּאָכע פֿון סאָציאַליסטישע רעוואָלוציעס—בעטן פֿרומע ייִדן, גאָט זאָל זיי באַגליקן, אַז זיי זאָלן ווידער קאָנען ברענגען קאָרבאַנעס [קרבנות]!

דורך אויסגעטראַכטע מייסעס [מעשיות] פֿון יעציעס־מיצראים [יציאת־מצרים], דורך דערצייִלונגען פֿון איבערנאַטירלעבע וווּנדער, אין וועלכע קיין איין געבילדעטער מענטש קאָן ניט גלויבן, ווייל ער וויסט די געזעצן פֿון דער נאַטור און די דערקלערונגען פֿון אירע דערשיינונגען, דורך פֿאַרשיידענע צערעמאָניעס, דינים, בראַכעס [ברכות] און טפֿילעס [תפילות] זוכט די קלעריקאַלע קאַסטע אייַנצוהאַלטן דעם גלויבן אין נאַציאָנאַלן גאָט.

צוזאַמען מיט דער ליבע און מוירע [מורא] פֿאַר דעם גאָט פֿון איסראָעל [ישראל] פֿלאַנצן זיי סינע [שינאה] און האַס צו אַלע אַנדערע פֿעלקער, וועלכע גלויבן ניט אין יהוה, און דינען אַנדערע געטער. ווען מע עפֿנט די טיר אין מיטן אָפּרייַבן דעם סיידער אויף אַרייַנצולאָזן עליאָהו־האַנאָווי [אליהו הנביא], פֿאַר וועלכן ס׳איז צוגעגרייט אַ באַזונדער בעכער ווייַן, בעטן די האַגאַדע־זאָגער [הגדה] זייער גאָט, ער זאָל אויסגיסן זיין קאַס [כעס] אויף די פֿעלקער, וואָס דינען אים ניט און זאָל זיי אין גאַנצן פֿאַרניכטן פֿון דער ערד.

Azoy flantst eyn di "heylike" Hagode libe tsum eygenem Got un sine tsu fremde mentshn.

Dos iz di oyfgabe fun yeder religye. In der mitsve tsu shpreytn sine tsvishn farsheydene felker shteyt nit op der rov funem pop, der pop funem ksyondz un der ksyondz funem male. Yeder fun zey dint tray zayn natsyonaln hershndikn ekspluatatorishn klas, un zey ale tsuzamen helfn, durkh farshpreytn fintsternish un umvisnheyt, eyntsuhitn di ekzistirndike ordenung fun eksplatatsye un knekhtshaft.

Dem yontev Peysekh, velkhn di Yidishe koyhanim un "khakhomim" hobn tsugegebn leponem a sheyn fun a frayheyt-yontev, hobn zey in der virklekhkeyt farvandlt in a yontev fun kamf kegn yeder bafrayungs-bavegung fun knekht kegn a hersher. In eyne fun di mayses vegn Yetsies-Mitsraim vert a file dertseylt vegn dem, az draysik toyznt Yidishe giboyrim fun di Bney-Efrayem hobn gevolt mit gever bafrayen zikh fun knekhtshaft, hot zey Got geshtroft, un zey zaynen oysgeharget gevorn derfar, vayl zey hobn zikh farlozn oyf di eygene koykhes un nit gevart biz Got aleyn vet zey bafrayen.

Gloybn in Got, farlozn zikh oyf zayn heylikn nomen, hofn oyf zayn gnod, vartn oyf zayne vunder, moyre hobn far zayn shtrof un libn im far zayn rakhmones, nit farlozn zikh oyf di eygene koykhes—dos iz der tsil fun di ale vunderlekhe mayses. Farshtarkn di libe tsum eygenem natsyonaln got un durkh dem farshtarkn di natsyonalistishe gefiln, shtern der fareynikung fun arbeter fun ale lender un natsyes in

אזוי פֿלאַנצט אײַן די ״הײליקע״ האַגאָדע [הגדה] ליבע צום אײגענעם גאָט
און שינאה [שינאה] צו פֿרעמדע מענטשן.

דאָס איז די אויפֿגאַבע פֿון יעדער רעליגיע. אין דער מיצווע [מיצוה]
צו שפּרײטן סינע [שינאה] צווישן פֿאַרשײדענע פֿעלקער שטײט ניט אָפּ
דער ראַוו [רב] פֿונעם פּאַפּ, דער פּאַפּ פֿונעם קסיאָנדז און דער קסיאָנדז
פֿונעם מולא [מאלע]. יעדער פֿון זײ דינט זיין נאַציאָנאַלן הערשנדיקן
עקספּלואַטאַטאָרישן קלאַס, און זײ אַלע צוזאַמען העלפֿן, דורך פֿאַרשפּרײטן
פֿינצטערניש און אומוויסנהייט, איינצוהיטן די עקזיסטירנדיקע אָרדענונג פֿון
עקספּלואַטאַציע און קנעכטשאַפֿט.

דעם יאָנטעוו [יום-טוב] פּײסעך [פסח], וועלכן די יידישע קויהאַנים
[כהנים] און ״באָכאָמים [חכמים]״ האָבן צוגעגעבן לעפּפֿאַנעם אַ שײן פֿון אַ
פֿרײהייט-יאָנטעוו [יום-טוב], האָבן זײ אין דער ווירקלעכקייט פֿאַרוואַנדלט
אין אַ יאָנטעוו [יום-טוב] פֿון קאַמף קעגן יעדער באַפֿרײונגס-באַוועגונג
פֿון קנעכט קעגן אַ הערשער. אין אײנע פֿון די מײסעס [מעשיות] וועגן
יעציעס-מיצראַעים [יציאת-מצרים] ווערט אַ פֿיל דערצײלט וועגן דעם, אז
דרײסיק טויזנט יידישע גיבוירים [גיבורים] פֿון די בני-עפֿראַעים [בני אפרים]
האָבן געוואַלט מיט געווער באַפֿרײען זיך פֿון קנעכטשאַפֿט, האָט זײ גאָט
געשטראָפֿט, און זײ זײנען אויסגעהאַרגעט [אויסגעהרגעט] געוואָרן דערפֿאַר,
ווײל זײ האָבן זיך פֿאַרלאָזן אויף די אײגענע קויכעס [כוחות] און ניט געוואַרט
ביז גאָט אַלײן וועט זײ באַפֿרײען.

גלויבן אין גאָט, פֿאַרלאָזן זיך אויף זיין הײליקן נאָמען, האָפֿן אויף זיין
גנאָד, וואַרטן אויף זיינע ווונדער, מוירע [מורא] האָבן פֿאַר זיין שטראָף און
ליבן אים פֿאַר זיין ראַכמאָנעס [רחמנות], ניט פֿאַרלאָזן זיך אויף די אײגענע
קויכעס—דאָס איז דער ציל פֿון די אַלע ווונדערלעכע מײסעס [מעשיות].
פֿאַרשטאַרקן די ליבע צום אײגענעם נאַציאָנאַלן גאָט און דורך דעם פֿאַרשטאַרקן
די נאַציאָנאַליסטישע געפֿילן, שטערן דער פֿאַרײניקונג פֿון אַרבעטער פֿון אַלע

kamf kegn zeyere unterdriker, preydikn di fareynikung fun ale klasn in eyn klal-Yisroel arum zeyer eygenem Got,—tsu dem shtrebn itst di Yidishe kley-koydesh, punkt vi di Zelbsthershung hot geshtrebt tsu fareynikn ale klasn fun Rusishn folk arum Pravoslavye.

A mayse fun frayheyt, kedey ayntsuhaltn lenger in knekht-shaft—dos iz di "Hagode shel Peysekh."

A legende vegn Gots shtarkeyt, vegn zayn almekhtikeyt, vunder un kuntsn, a loybgezang Gots koyekh un a farurteylung fun dem mentshns zelbstetikayt un zayn frayheyts-kamf—iz di mayse fun Yetiyes-Mitsraim!

Nit keyn frayheyt-yontev, nor a yontev fun gaystiker farshklafung iz Peysekh. Mir darfn azelkhe yontoyvim nit hobn. Mir fayern unzere proletarishe, revolutsyonere emese frayheyt-yontoyvim, ven dos folk aleyn hot oyfgevakht fun shlof, in velkhn s'hobn es farvigt Gots diner; ven es hot tserisn di keytn fun knekhtshaft un ekspluatatsye, in velkhe s'hobn es farshmidt zayne unterdriker—kapitalistn un pritsim; ven der arbeter-klas aleyn iz mit gever in hant aroysgetrotn als der eygener bafrayer fun zayn klas, **ven er hot zikh opgezogt fun der oysgetrakhter natsyonaler eynheyt tsulib der proletarisher akhdes fun ale lender un felker.**

Ven mir fayern unzere revolutsyonere yontoyvim, farnemen mir zikh nit mit azelkhe kluge pshetlekh vi Rebe Yehuda, Rebe Yosi Haglili,

לענדער און נאַציעס אין קאַמף קעגן זייערע אונטערדריקער, פֿאַריידיקן די פֿאַרייניקונג פֿון אלע קלאסן אין איין קלאל-איסראעל [כלל-ישראל] אַרום זייער אייגענעם גאָט,—צו דעם שטרעבן איצט די ייִדישע קליי-קוידעש [כלי-קודש], פּונקט ווי די זעלבסטהערשונג האָט געשטערעבט צו פֿאַרייניקן אלע קלאסן פֿון רוסישן פֿאָלק אַרום פּראוואָסלאַוויע.

אַ מײַסע [מעשׂה] פֿון פֿרייהייט, קעדיי [כדי] אײַנצוהאַלטן לענגער אין קנעכטשאַפֿט—דאָס איז די ,,האַגאדע שעל פּייסעך [הגדה של פסח]."

אַ לעגענדע וועגן גאָטס שטאַרקייט, וועגן זײַן אַלמעכטיקייט, ווונדער און קונצן, אַ לויבגעזאַנג גאָטס קוייעך [כוח] און אַ פֿאַראורטיילונג פֿון דעם מענטשנס זעלבסטעמיקייט און זײַן פֿרייהייטס-קאַמף—איז די מײַסע [מעשׂה] פֿון יעציעס-מיצראַיִם [יציאת-מצרים]!

ניט קיין פֿרייהייט-יאָנטעוו [יום-טוב], נאָר אַ יאָנטעוו [יום-טוב] פֿון גייסטיקער פֿאַרשקלאַפֿונג איז פּייסעך [פסח]. מיר דאַרפֿן אזעלכע יאָנטוייווים [יום-טובים] ניט האָבן. מיר פֿײַערן אונזערע פּראַלעטאַרישע, רעוואָלוציאָנערע עמעסע פֿרייהייט-יאָנטוייווים [יום-טובים], ווען דאָס פֿאָלק אַליין האָט אויפֿגעוואַכט פֿון שלאָף, אין וועלכע ס׳האָבן עס פֿאַרוויגט גאָטס דינער; ווען עס האָט צעריסן די קייטן פֿון קנעכטשאַפֿט און עקספּלואָטאַציע, אין וועלכע ס׳האָבן עס פֿאַרשמידט זײַנע אונטערדריקער—קאַפּיטאַליסטן און פּריצים; ווען דער אַרבעטער-קלאַס אַליין איז מיט געוואָר אין האָט אַרויסגעטראָטן אלס דער אייגענער באַפֿרײַער פֿון זײַן קלאַס, ווען ער האָט זיך אָפּגעזאָגט פֿון דער אויסגעטראַכטער נאַציאָנאַלער איינהייט צוליב דער פּראַלעטאַרישער אַכדעם [אחדות] פֿון אלע לענדער און פֿעלקער.

ווען מיר פֿײַערן אונזערע רעוואָלוציאָנערע יאָנטוייווים [יום-טובים], פֿאַרנעמען מיר זיך ניט מיט אזעלכע קלוגע פּשעטלעך [פּשטלעך] ווי רבי

Rebe Elyezer un Rebe Akiva vegn di makes, vos Got hot geshikt oyf di Mitsrim. Di kluge rabonim ampern zikh vegn dem, vifl makes hot geshikt Gots finger un vifl zayn gantse hant; vifl makes hot er geshikt oyf der yaboshe un vifl oyfn yam, un vifl danken darf der Yid gebn dem Reboyne-shel-oylem far yeder Mitsrayemsher make,—mir dertseyln oyf unzere yontoyvim.

Vi shver un dorndik iz der veg fun kamf far frayheyt, vifl unzere beste khaveyrim zaynen umgekumen in di turmes un oyf di tlyes in dem tsarishn Rusland un kumen nokh itst um in di "demokratishe" lender fun Eyrope un Amerike. Vi shtandhaftik un heldnmutik der proletaryat kemft far zayn frayheyt, velkhe partey hot im gefirt in kamf un hot im ongevizn di rikhtike vegn fun bafrayung, un velkhe hot im farratn un ibergegebn in di hent fun zayne sonim. **Mir batrakhtn dem durkhgegangenem veg fun kamf, shatsn op unzere rikhtike kamf-mitlen, farurteyln unzere felern un nemen on mitlen, zey zoln nit ibergekhazert vern.**

Mir dertseyln oykh vegn di makes, **vos di burzhuazye hot geshikt oyfn kemfndikn proletaryat:**

Milyukov, Tshernov, Krasnov, Kornilov, Kerenski, Tshaikovski, Hots, Petlyure, Denikin, Vrangel, Makhno, Pilsudski, Sheydeman, Noske, Vandervelde.

Nit tsen, nor hunderter azelkhe makes! Mir dertseyln vegn di

יהודא, רבי יוסי הגלילי, רבי אליעזער און רבי עקיבא וועגן די מאקעס [מכות], וואָס גאָט האָט געשיקט אויף די מיצרים. די קלוגע ראַבאָנים [רבנים] אַמפּערן זיך וועגן דעם, וויפֿל מאקעס [מכות] האָט געשיקט גאָטס פֿינגער און וויפֿל זיין גאנצע האנט; וויפֿל מאקעס [מכות] האָט ער געשיקט אויף דער יאבאשע [יבשה] און וויפֿל אויפֿן ים [ים], און וויפֿל דאנקען דארף דער ייִד געבן דעם רעבוינע־שעל־אוילעם [רבונו־של־עולם] פֿאַר יעדער מיצראיעמשער מאקע [מכה],—מיר דערציילן אויף אונזערע יאָנטויוויים [יום־טובֿים].

ווי שווער און דאָרנדיק איז דער וועג פֿון קאַמף פֿאַר פֿרייהייט, וויפֿל אונזערע בעסטע כאווייריס [חברים] זיינען אומגעקומען אין די טורמעס און אויף די טליעס [תליות] אין דעם צאַרישן רוסלאַנד און קומען נאָך איצט אום אין די „דעמאָקראַטישע" לענדער פֿון אייראָפּע און אמעריקע. ווי שטאַנדהאַפֿטיק און העלדנמוטיק דער פּראָלעטאַריאט קעמפֿט פֿאַר זיין פֿרייהייט, וועלכע פּאַרטיי האָט אים געפֿירט אין קאַמף און האָט אים אָנגעוויזן די ריכטיקע וועגן פֿון באַפֿרייונג, און וועלכע האָט אים פֿאַרראַטן און איבערגעגעבן אין די הענט פֿון זיינע סאָנים [שונאים]. מיר באַטראַכטן דעם דורכגעגאַנגענעם וועג פֿון קאַמף, שאַצן אָפּ אונזערע ריכטיקע קאַמף־מיטלען, פֿאַראורטיילן אונזערע פֿעלערן און נעמען אן מיטלען, זיי זאָלן ניט איבערגעכאַזערט [איבערגעחזרט] ווערן.

מיר דערציילן אויך וועגן די מאקעס [מכות], וואָס די בורזשואַזיע האָט געשיקט אויפֿן קעמפֿנדיקן פּראָלעטאַריאט:

מיליוקאָוו, טשערנאָוו, קראסנאָוו, קאָרנילאָוו, קערענסקי, טשאַיקאָווסקי, האָץ, פֿעטליורע, דעניקין, וואראַנגעל, מאַכנאָ, פּילסודסקי, סיידעמאַן, נאָסקע, וואַנדערוועלדע.

ניט צען, נאָר הונדערטער אזעלבע מאַקעס [מכות]! מיר דערציילן וועגן

makes un vayzn on: **di make iz fun der Kadetisher Partey, di—fun der Eserisher, yene—fun Menshevikes un di—fun PPS.** Eyne fun zey iz oyfn kontrrevolutsyoner, di andere—farshleyert unter a dektukh fun sotsyalizm un demokratye, un ale tsuzamen—glaykhe sonim fun arbeter-klas. **Mir vayzn on, vu zaynen unzere sonim un vu zaynen unzere fraynd. Mir makhn a sakhakl fun unzer fargangener revolutsyonerer tetikeyt un merkn on di vegn fun vayterdikn kamf.**

Anshtot Kries-Yamsuf, dertseyln mir vegn der heldisher gvure fun der Royter Armey ba **Perekop**. Anshtot di krekhtsn fun di Yidn in Mitsraim un Gots vunder, dertseyln mir di virklekhe laydn fun proletaryat un poyertum in zeyer oyfshtand kegn zeyere unterdriker, zeyer heldishn kamf un rumfuln zig.

Anshtot tsu dertseyln di vunder, vi Got hot geboyt zayn Beys-Habkhire, zayn Beys-Hamikdesh in Yerusholaim—dertseyln mir vi der proletaryat fun FSSR boyt dem sotsyalizm, in land fun emeser frayheyt un glaykhheyt far ale arbetndike fun ale felker, un mir rufn ale arbeter un poyerim tsu nemen an aktivn onteyl in der grandyezer boyung.

Kont ir itst farglaykhn, khaveyrim, dem rabonishn Peysekh tsum proletarishn Ershtn May, di oysgetrakhte mayse fun Yetsies-Mitsraim tsu der proletarisher Oktober-Revolutsye?

Efnt oyf khaveyrim di toyern fun der proletarisher melukhe un

די מאקעס און ווייזן אן: די מאקע [מכּה] איז פֿון דער קאַדעטישער פּאַרטיי, די—פֿון דער עסערישער, יענע—פֿון מענשעוויקעס און די—פֿון פּ.פּ.ס. איינע פֿון זיי איז אויפֿן קאָנטררעוואָלוציאָנער, די אַנדערע—פֿאַרשלייערט אונטער אַ דעקטוך פֿון סאָציאַליזם און דעמאָקראַטיע, און אַלע צוזאַמען—גלייבע סאָנים [שׂונאים] פֿון אַרבעטער־קלאַס. מיר ווייזן אן, וווּ זיינען אונזערע סאָנים [שׂונאים] און וווּ זיינען אונזערע פֿריינד. מיר מאַכן אַ סאַבאַקל [סך־הכּל] פֿון אונזער פֿאַרגאַנגענער רעוואָלוציאָנערער טעטיקייט און מערקן אָן די וועגן פֿון ווייטערדיקן קאַמף.

אַנשטאַט קריעס־יאַמסוף [קריעת־ים־סוף], דערציילן מיר וועגן דער העלדישער גוווּרע [גבֿורה] פֿון דער רויטער אַרמיי ביי פּערעקאָפּ. אַנשטאַט די קרעכצן פֿון די יידן אין מיצראַים [מצרים] און גאָטס וווּנדער, דערציילן מיר די ווירקלעכע ליידן פֿון פּראָלעטאַריאַט און פּויערטום אין זייער אויפֿשטאַנד קעגן זייערע אונטערדריקער, זייער העלדישן קאַמף און רומפֿולן זיג.

אַנשטאַט צו דערציילן די וווּנדער, ווי גאָט האָט געבויט זיין בייס־האַבבירע [בית־הבּחירה], זיין בייס־האַמיקדעש [בית־המיקדש] אין יערושאַלאַים [ירושלים]—דערציילן מיר ווי דער פּראָלעטאַריאַט פֿון פּ.ס.ס.ר. בויט דעם סאָציאַליזם, אין לאַנד פֿון עמעסער פֿרייהייט און גלייכהייט פֿאַר אַלע אַרבעטנדיקע פֿון אַלע פֿעלקער, און מיר רופֿן אַלע אַרבעטער און פּויערים צו נעמען אַן אַקטיוון אָנטייל אין דער גראַנדיעוזער בויונג.

קאָנט איר איצט פֿאַרגלייכן, כאַוויירים [חבֿרים], דעם ראַבאַנישן [רבנישן] פּייסעך [פּסח] צום פּראָלעטאַרישן ערשטן מיי, די אויסגעטראַכטע מייסע [מעשׂה] פֿון יעציעס־מיצראַים [יציאת־מצרים] צו דער פּראָלעטאַרישער אָקטאָבער־רעוואָלוציע?

עפֿנט אויף כאַוויירים [חבֿרים] די טויערן פֿון דער פּראָלעטאַרישער

vayzt ale arbeter un poyerim fun der gantser velt, vos gefinen zikh nokh untern yokh fun kapital, vi mir hobn far unzer frayheyt gekemft, un vi mir hobn di makht in unzere eygene hent genumen. Ruft tsu ale arbeter fun der gantser velt: Shteyt oyf kegn ayere sonim! Bafrayt zikh fun ayere farreter! Kumt tsuzamen mit unz, unter der onfirung fun Komunistishn Internatsyonal, in antsheydenem kamf kegn der kapitalistisher velt!

Derbay makht, khaveyrim.

מעלוכע [מלוכה] און װײזט אַלע אַרבעטער און פּױערים פֿון דער גאַנצער װעלט, װאָס געפֿינען זיך נאָך אונטערן יאָך פֿון קאַפּיטאַל, װי מיר האָבן פֿאַר אונזער פֿרײהײט געקעמפֿט, און װי מיר האָבן די מאַכט אין אונזערע אײגענע הענט גענומען. רופֿט צו אַלע אַרבעטער פֿון דער גאַנצער װעלט: שטײט אױף קעגן אײערע סאָנים [שׂונאים]! באַפֿרײַט זיך פֿון אײערע פֿאַרדרעטער! קומט צוזאַמען מיט אונז, אונטער דער אָנפֿירונג פֿון קאָמוניסטישן אינטערנאַציאָנאַל, אין אַנטשײדנעם קאַמף קעגן דער קאַפּיטאַליסטישער װעלט!

דערבײ מאַכט, כּאַװײרים [חבֿרים].

Koyrekh

Leygt tsunoyf dem Tsveytn Internatsyonal mit der Felker-Lige, tsvishn zey leygt arayn dem Tsionizm un zogt "yokhluhu," zol zey oyfesn der alveltlekher revolutsyonerer oyfshtand fun proletaryat.

קוירעך [כריך]

לייגט צונויף דעם צוויטן אינטערנאַציאָנאַל מיט דער פֿעלקער-ליגע, צווישן זיי לייגט אַריין דעם ציאָניזם [ציוניזם] און זאָגט ,,יאַכלוהו'', זאָל זיי אויפֿעסן דער אַלוועלטלעכער רעוואָלוציאָנערער אויפֿשטאַנד פֿון פּראָלעטאַריאַט.

Halel

Zing dem "Internatsyonal"
Un zog:

Nider mitn shiml fun doyres!
Nider mit di klerikale natsyonalistishe yontoyvim!
Zoln lebn di revolutsyonere arbeter-yontoyvim!

האַלעל [הלל]

זינג דעם „אינטערנאַציאָנאַל"
און זאָג:

נידער מיטן שימל פֿון דוירעס [דורות]!
נידער מיט די קלעריקאַלע נאַציאָנאַליסטישע יאָנטוייווים [יום־טובים]!
זאָלן לעבן די רעוואָלוציאָנערע אַרבעטער־יאָנטוייווים [יום־טובים]!

www.ingramcontent.com/pod-product-compliance
Lightning Source LLC
LaVergne TN
LVHW092054060526
838201LV00047B/1388